FORM 19

FISCHLER'S
ILLUSTRATED

HISTORY
of
HOCKEY

FISCHLER'S ILLUSTRATED
HISTORY of HOCKEY

STAN FISCHLER

Warwick Publishing Inc.
Toronto   Los Angeles

Fischler's Illustrated History of Hockey

Copyright © 1993 Stan Fischler

Published by the Warwick Publishing Group
Warwick Publishing Inc., 24 Mercer Street, Toronto, Ontario M5V 1H3
Warwick Publishing Inc., 1300 N. Alexandria, Los Angeles, California 90027

Cover Design: Dave Hader
Cover Photos: Harold Barkley, Steve Hutchinson,
Text Design: Nick Pitt

ISBN 1-895629-21-7

Distributed in North America by:
Firefly Books Ltd.
250 Sparks Avenue
Willowdale, Ontario
M2H 2S4

Printed and bound in Canada.

To Simon, who wrote his own bit of history in 1993.

Hockey's greatest goaltender — Terry Sawchuk — in his prime.

Contents

Acknowledgements

A number of people helped make this book possible with diligent research, office help, and innumerable other forms of assistance. The debt to them is immense and thanks infinite.

They include Craig Levitt, Susanna Mandel-Montello, Eric Servetah, Dan Hurwitz, Ashley Scharge, Mark Platt, Joel Bergman, Lisa Chenier, Todd Diamond, Randy Hu, Sandra MacPherson, Mary McCarthy, Matt Messina, Alan Rozinsky, Scott Tracht, Brian McDonough, Keith Drabik, Tony Hamilton, Rick Sorci, Joe Aguiar, Mike Hersch, Trinity Mills, Jim Ramsey, Dan Carle, Rob Daley, Ira Sheier, Sean Farrel, Richard Middleton, Diane Gerace, Marc Cochrane, Jeff Silverstein, Al Goldfarb, Thomas Losier, Jeff Clarke, James DeMelo, Chris Lemon, John Ploszay and Alexia Demitriou.

Introduction

THE HOCKEY REVOLUTION IS NOW. We have the Mighty Ducks of Anaheim, the Panthers of South Florida — Disney and Blockbuster Video in the NHL. And would you believe a major league club in Dallas called the Stars?

Egad, Lord Stanley of Preston surely must be looking down from above with a mixture of awe and amusement.

Yes, Canada's national pastime has travelled light years since the frigid prairie afternoons when homesteaders faced off with hickory branches and stickhandled frozen cow dung across a pond.

In time we had the Ottawa Silver Seven, the Portage La Prairie Terriers, Cyclone Taylor, Newsy Lalonde, the Vancouver Millionaires, Hoby Baker, the St. Nicholas Club, Bad Joe Hall, and the Seattle Metropolitans.

And I'll bet you that Eric Lindros has never heard of George Hainsworth, Lorne Chabot, Frank Patrick or even Joe Malone, who Eric the large occasionally resembles.

Which is another way of saying that hockey's rich history is too often ignored by contemporary fans and even players. Whatever the reasons, this *Illustrated History of Hockey* attempts to bring to life everything of importance about our favorite sport. In plain English, I've tried to tell you about everyone from Georges Vezina to Ed Belfour — with Sweeney Shriner thrown in for good measure.

I hope you enjoy reading about it as much as I enjoyed writing about them.

On to the opening faceoff!

Stan Fischler
New York, New York
August, 1993

CHAPTER ONE

Humble Beginnings

IF YOU HAD A DOLLAR for every theory about hockey's origins, you could buy yourself a brand new Rolls-Royce.

Theories on the game's roots are as plentiful as Arctic snow; and just as difficult to plow through without exertion.

Suffice to say that there abound both logical and illogical ideas, some of which will be examined here.

One respected school of thought has it that hockey can be traced to the British Isles and France. In Scotland, field hockey was popular but called "shinny," a term that has carried down to the present game. In the 16th century, the Irish referred to it as "hurley" and in France it was known as "hocquet."

When the cold winter winds froze European ponds and lakes, it was only natural for the hurley and hocquet players to move on to the ice and adapt their summer pastime for the cold months. There was no rubber puck, as we know it today, but there were brass balls which could be batted around with weighty shillelaghs.

As for the first skates, again, there are several schools of thought about their origins in the British Isles. What is known is that the English marshlands community of Bury Fen frequently was pelted with heavy rains during the late fall. When the flat meadows were covered with shallow water, a sudden freeze would inspire the citizens of Bury Fen to skitter around the ice in one of the more primitive versions of hockey, which then was called "bandy."

The natives of Bury Fen became quite adept at their game by the 1820s and eventually played matches against teams from nearby towns. In lieu of a puck, the English used a wooden or cork ball, sometimes called a "kit" or "cat." In time it was replaced with a rubberized replica.

Not long afterward, Hollanders perfected a metal blade that could be attached to a shoe and with the invention of the practical ice skate, hockey couldn't be far behind.

Sticks were another story; a far cry from the aluminum shafted implements of the 1990s. Natives of Bury Fen searched for branches of the pollard willow trees which were common in the area. The branch was trimmed so that it

One of the earliest hockey heros, Hobey Baker was an American hero in WWI whose career ended in a fatal plane crash in 1917. (Opposite) Baker starred for the Princeton team early in the century.

had a blade of sorts and often was so durable that players would occasionally pass their sticks down to offspring.

The origins of hockey in North America are more easily traceable but, again, there are to this day arguments about the precise location of the first games although several communities — Kingston, Halifax and Montreal — each were sites of early organized games.

Kingston's most emphatic claim was made in the late 19th Century by James T. (Captain Jim) Sutherland whose research determined that

North America's first hockey league was launched there in 1885. Sutherland spoke firsthand, having played for a club called the Athletics in the four-team league which included the Kingstons, Royal Military College and Queens University.

According to Captain Jim, Queens University defeated the Athletics, 3-1, to capture the first Canadian League title. Sutherland and others wore an improved skate with a "spring" that clamped the blade to one's boot. But, as Captain Jim recalled, it did present problems:

HOBART EMORY HARE "*Hobey*" BAKER

To the memory of a gentleman, scholar, and athlete whose brilliant play and sportsmanship made him America's hockey immortal.

"In one game our goalie was using his skates to block the ice-hugging shots," Sutherland remembered. "The impact would release the trigger-type fastener of the skate and the skate would fly off the goalie's boot and go sailing across the rink."

Like Kingston, Halifax has substantive claims to early versions of hockey — if not the earliest — based on games played by British soldiers who were posted to bases in and around the city, starting in 1870.

Montreal's major hockey impetus began with construction of covered skating rinks whose original purpose was to provide ice for recreational skaters but eventually was also used for hockey.

Victoria Skating Rink became a center for McGill University students in Downtown Montreal and in 1875 they played a game with nine players on each side. One hockey historian, Neil Isaacs of the University of Maryland, established that the first codified set of hockey rules were the product of McGill players, W.F. Robertson and R.F. Smith, in 1879.

Refinements to the game came swiftly. The nine-man game gave way to the seven-man game late in the 19th century when one of the clubs showed up for the 1886 Montreal Winter Carnival short a pair of players. The other team obliged by dropping two of its skaters and the trimmed roster proved suitable to both sides. Suddenly, seven-man hockey became de rigeueur.

During that same epoch, the ball gave way to the puck and the field hockey stick, then in common use, was refined so that players could dribble the puck with either side of the stick blade. As the game moved from the outdoors to indoor rinks, snowbanks, which measured the perimeter along the makeshift river games, disappeared in favor of formal sideboards, forty inches high.

A Montreal sportswriter named Arthur Farrell, who also was a member of the Montreal Shamrock Hockey Club, is credited with arranging an early set of rules that certified, among other things, a seven-man game, six-by-four-feet goal dimensions, and a rink that would measure approximately 112 feet long by 58 feet wide.

An itinerant Montrealer, T.L. Patton ventured to Toronto in the late 1880s and told his Ontario pals about hockey's growth and virtues. A goaltender, Patton was so persuasive, he convinced Torontonians to obtain stickhandling equipment and soon the Granites, St. George's and the Toronto Athletic Club emerged as significant teams.

It was only natural that once organized leagues sprouted in these cities that interurban games would be played. Before very long keen rivalries were established between teams in Toronto, Ottawa, and Montreal.

In terms of the game's more formal organization, the year 1892 generally is regarded as the landmark date if for no other reason than the donation of a then modest piece of silverware which would, in time, gain international renown.

When the Earl of Derby, Lord Stanley of Preston, became governor general of Canada, he could not have even remotely imagined the result of his passing interest in a wintry game.

Lord Stanley's fascination with hockey happened more because of his sons than the governor general himself. Arthur and Algernon Stanley skated on an outdoor rink which had been constructed and flooded by servants outside Government House (Rideau Hall). The Stanley boys encouraged members of the local militia, the Coldstream Guards, to play with them and even dubbed the club the Rideau Rebels.

In time the Rebels challenged other teams

including the powerful Ottawa City Club and while his sons chased the elusive puck, Lord Stanley was chasing an idea planted by his aide, Lord Kilcoursie, who also played for the Rebels — why not strike a trophy for the best hockey team in the entire Dominion?

The governor general agreed with the proposal and offered ten guineas ($48.67 in Canadian cash) for the silver bowl with the interior gold finish. It was purchased by Lord Stanley's sidekick, Captain Charles Colville, on a trip to Great Britain. Since there were only amateur teams in Canada at the time, the recipient would remain for some time within the province of those who considered hockey a labor of love.

Ironically, Lord Stanley returned to his English home before the first Cup was up for competition in 1893 and won by the Montreal Amateur Athletic Association's team. It was the first of seven straight Amateur Hockey Association of Canada championships for the club nicknamed the Winged Wheelers because of the emblem on their sweaters.

The Montrealers won The Cup a second time in 1894 but confusion reigned a year later after the Winged Wheelers lost the league championship to the cross town Montreal Victorias. However, The Stanley Cup was designed as a challenge trophy and the Montreal AAA, which still held the Cup, was challenged by a team from Queen's University. The Wheelers won, 5-1, but the Victorias were awarded The Cup having annexed the league championship.

By this time organized hockey had significantly spread west across the Dominion and a Winnipeg club, also called the Victorias, issued a challenge to their Montreal namesakes. This was something of a surprise since Easterners still considered themselves masters of the ice game.

However, on February 14, 1896, the Winnipeg and Montreal Victorias played in Mon-

Herb Gallagher of Northwestern University was another early hockey hero who's career was interrupted by WWI. He later went on to become Athletic Director at Northwestern.

treal and, to the astonishment of many, Winnipeg triumphed 2-0. A return match was played on December 30, 1896 in Winnipeg and, this time, Montreal regained The Cup with a 6-5 comeback victory.

While all this was going on, the technique of playing the game continually was refined. Winnipeg's goalie introduced cricket pads to the equipment repertoire and this inspired other netminders to adopt the protective device. The face-off continued evolving from the "bully" system of field hockey (two players facing each other and then banging sticks together three times before play) to a method (at referee's signal, the players went after the puck) closer to the present system. Shooting the puck, which was extraordinarily basic at the beginning, be-

came refined when the Winnipeggers introduced the "scoop" (later to be known as the
wrist) shot.

The seven man game now was universal.
It comprised the goaltender, two defensemen,
three forwards and a rover. Before the turn of
the century, the defensemen were known as
the point and cover point and stood in front of
each other rather than side by side as is the
mode in contemporary hockey. The rover had
the option of moving up with the attack or back
with the defenders.

Goaltending restrictions were imposed and
— incredibly, in view of today's game — goalies were penalized if they deliberately fell to
the ice to block the puck. Onside play, which
meant no forward passing, was developed in
Quebec and approved throughout and lifting
of the puck, unknown at first, became fashionable and approved by rule makers.

Not surprisingly, the popularity of hockey
had swiftly spread south of the Canadian border although the Americans had originally preferred a version called "ice polo," (a five-man
game played with a rubber ball) that soon was
eschewed for the Canadian brand.

Perhaps the most meaningful early contribution of the American skaters came from an

*Left: One of the father's of hockey in
America, George Brown helped build
the Boston arena in 1910 and organized the Boston Athletic Association
Hockey Team. The BAA developed
into a power in International hockey
(amateur) and competed with top
ranking college and club teams from
across North America. Brown created
the base of interest in the sport that
enabled professional hockey to thrive
in beantown.*

*Opposite: Hockey's first dynasty, the
Ottawa Siver Seven, shown here with
the Stanley Cup in 1902. The Silver
Seven won the cup three seasons in a
row, from 1902 to 1905. The team
was led by Frank McGee (standing,
far right), who was the greatest
player of the age.*

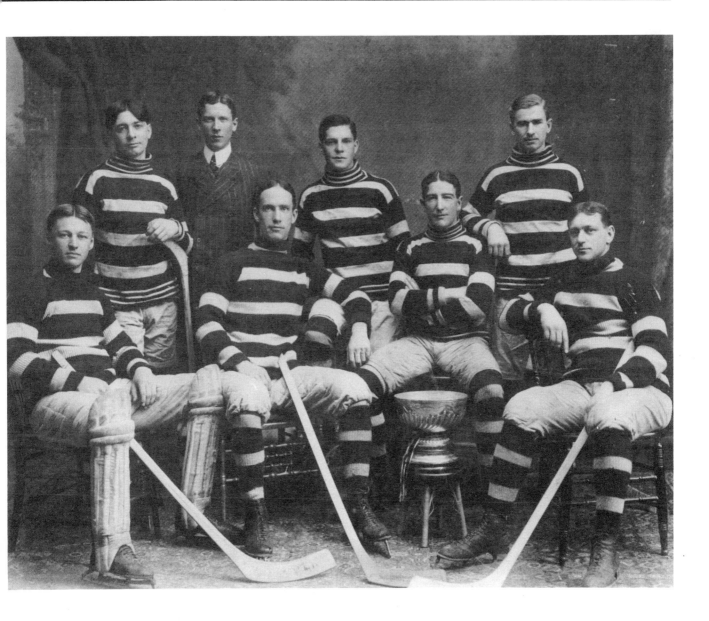

Illinois ice polo contingent who ventured to Ontario for an exhibition series. Rather than employ the traditional posts-in-ice to mark the goal, the Americans used a cage which proved so popular that what we now know as the goal net became part of the hockey scene.

Because of the climate differential, hockey playing on outdoor rinks was more limited in the United States which explains why the first artificial ice arenas sprouted in American cities before they did in Canada.

The first to appear in New York City was the St. Nicholas Arena near Central Park and Times Square. Its promoters invited the Stanley Cup champion Montreal Wanderers and the Ottawa Senators to Manhattan for a two-game exhibition series which captured the imagination of New Yorkers.

If hockey could make it on Broadway — which it did, to rave reviews — it could make it anywhere and, from the early 1900s on, the stickhandling boom evolved in a chain reaction of fits and bursts. More than anything, the introduction of professionals on to the hitherto all-amateur scene would dramatically and forever alter hockey's fabric.

CHAPTER TWO
The Pros Take Over

SURPRISINGLY, although the best hockey players were being developed in Canada, the first professional hockey league was organized in the United States. Even more unlikely is the fact that it was conceived by a dentist, one Dr. J.L. Gibson in Houghton, Michigan.

The date was 1904 and the venue was the copper-mining area of Michigan's Upper Peninsula. The International Pro Hockey League, as it was called, featured Canadian pro stars, spread over teams through the frigid Michigan communities. Houghton's own club, the Portage Lakes, had Dr. Gibson, himself, on defense and dominated the league in its brief existence through 1907.

From time to time, the Portage Lakers would take to barnstorming and defeated such

Opposite: Hockey's first professional star was Fred "Cyclone" Taylor who made headlines in the early 1900s. A remarkable skater, Taylor played at both ends of the continent including exhibition games in New York City in 1910 and 1911. Here he is seen in a Vancouver uniform late in his career.

formidable squads as the Pittsburgh Bankers, St.Paul Victorias and the Montreal Wanderers. This was possible because the Portage Lake lineup was sprinkled with such Hall of Famers as Riley Hern, Cyclone Taylor, Hod Stuart and "Bad" Joe Hall, each of whom would be heard from in the decade to come.

Unfortunately, the towns supporting the teams — Houghton had fewer than 4,000 citizens — were too small to sustain the professionals on a long-term basis, particularly since the larger cities began widening their hockey horizons.

The benchmark for North American pro hockey was 1910 with the emergence of the National Hockey Association and the infusion of big money into the game. Such teams as the Montreal Wanderers, Renfrew Millionaires and, soon, the Montreal Canadiens, were to have major impact and, in no time at all, the brothers Lester and Frank Patrick had organized the Pacific Coast League on the other side of the nation.

Before the Canadiens blossomed into Cana-

Left: Frank Frederickson, out of Winnipeg, was a WWI ace who went on to star for the Victoria Cougars. They won the Stanley Cup in 1924.

Below: Before they became the Maple Leafs, Toronto's NHL representative was the St. Patricks. The club's most glamorous star was Cecil "Babe" Dye.

da's premier team, the Ottawa Senators were regarded as la creme de la creme of pro hockey, and for good reason. The Senators' goalkeeper Percy Lesueur, as well as Jack Darragh, Marty Walsh and Bruce Ridpath were among the best in Canada, guiding Ottawa to a 1911 Stanley Cup triumph after fending off challenges from Galt (7-4) and Port Arthur (13-4).

In October 1911 the NHA made what was to be a momentous decision when it eliminated the rover position and reduced the number of players on the ice to one goaltender and five skaters. The only trouble was that the Pacific Coast League refused to conform and, as a result, the two organizations would be at odds over this rule every time they competed against each other, which was often.

Quebec, which was fast becoming a hockey center, annexed its first Stanley Cup in 1912. Bad Joe Hall surfaced once again among the Bulldogs' aces along with Harry Mummery and

Joe Malone, the latter of whom would become one of pro hockey's most productive forwards.

With each season, the Stanley Cup gained more lustre but it wasn't until 1914 when a transcontinental series finally was arranged between the NHA titlists and their Pacific Coast League counterparts. By that time the amateurs had concentrated their attention on the Allan Cup as emblematic of Canada's senior (amateur) champions while the NHA-PCHL combine persuaded the Stanley Cup trustees that the silverware should be competed for by the play-for-pay stickhandlers.

Another milestone was achieved in 1914 when the Toronto Blueshirts hosted the Montreal Canadiens. Heretofore, all Stanley Cup matches had been played on natural ice but this time the teams had the benefit of artificial ice in Toronto, a first in Cup play.

The Blueshirts remained a pro hockey power until 1916 when Toronto was beset with the kind of free agent competition that has afflicted champions to this day. The chief reason for Toronto's downfall was a salary war that developed between the Pacific Coast Hockey Association and the NHA, principally because a new Seattle franchise was desperate for players. Soon after Cully Wilson of Toronto "jumped" to Seattle prior to the 1916 season, he was followed by Frank Foyston and other stars.

Meanwhile, World War I had exploded across Europe and Canada quickly became one of the primary suppliers of manpower for the Allied Forces. This automatically meant that talent would be diminished in both quantity and quality across the Dominion although the situation never was severe enough to result in a cessation of play.

While the NHA remained an exclusively Canadian-based league, the PCHL embraced two American cities, Portland and Seattle, both of which iced formidable teams. In 1917 the

Above: Ever since their inception, the Montreal Canadiens were identified as the team that represented French Canada. One of their foremost stars was Didier Pitre. Note that this shot was taken beore the club switched to the now famous Club de Hockey Canadien logo (see next page).

Seattle Metropolitans defeated the Canadiens, becoming the first U.S. team to take home Lord Stanley's silverware.

If that was not a momentous enough event, another would have much longer-range repercussions — creation of the National Hockey League!

The metamorphosis from NHA to NHL produced backroom melodramatics that would have made for gripping theater. Act I took place

It was fashionable in the early 1920s for players to pose outside the dressing room door for publicity shots.

These two classic shots are of Georges Vezina (right) and Didier Pitre (below), both taken outside the Montreal Forum.

Known as the "Chicoutimi Cucumber," Vezina was hockey's greatest goalie until he died suddenly of tuberculosis in 1926. The Vezina Trophy, named in his honour, is awarded to the NHL's best goalie each season.

during the summer of 1917 when NHA owners scanned their rosters and realized that too many good players had been lost to the war effort and serious talk about dropping pro hockey for the duration was heard in many board rooms.

When the NHA convened for its annual meeting, November 17, 1917, the Quebec franchise announced that it was dropping out of the NHA. That bombshell was followed by a series of emergency meetings designed to save the NHA from complete disaster. The Quebec announcement detonated two more "crash" meetings with leaders of the Ottawa, Toronto, Canadiens and Montreal Wanderers franchises debating the league's future.

In a curious turnabout, the governors decided to scrap the NHA altogether and construct a brand new league with the same teams.

Thus, on November 26, 1917, at the Windsor Hotel in downtown Montreal, the NHL was officially created. Only one aspect was different; ownership of the Toronto franchise. In what developed into a brief executive merry-go-round, Charles Querrie first annexed, then lost, then again annexed the managership of the Toronto sextet, emerging with full power to hire and fire players.

Once Quebec announced its abandonment of pro hockey, the entire roster of the dissolved team was put up for sale in a modified form of a draft system. This produced the second shock of the still unplayed 1917-18 season when the Canadiens obtained from Quebec both Joe Malone and Bad Joe Hall, two of the better professionals in Canada.

"Joe might have been the most prolific scorer of all time if they had played more games in those days," said Frank J. Selke, the former Canadiens' managing director who saw Malone play as a young pro. "It was amazing the way Joe used to get himself in position to score."

Malone was the NHL's first superstar, giving the baby league the kind of lustre Wayne Gretzky would 70 years later. When the Canadiens obtained Malone for the 1917-18 season, they instantly became a force.

"Quite often," Malone remembered, "I played fifty or fifty-five minutes a game. They didn't bother too much about changing lines, only individuals. There were only about nine or ten players on each team. I used to stick-handle in close and beat the goalie with a wrist shot. There was no forward passing allowed in the offensive zone and not as much scrambling as there is today. We wore shoulder and elbow pads, but the equipment wasn't too heavy and this was a good thing considering the number of minutes we had to play each game.

"The goalkeepers stood up a lot more. Vezina was a wonderful stand-up goalie who used to stop most shots with his stick. George Hainsworth and Paddy Moran were other good ones. There were no slapshots, but much more passing and stick-handling than today."

Malone's most notable achievement, which came later, was his record-breaking achievement of seven goals in a game scored on the night of January 31, 1920, in Quebec City. Three of the goals were scored within two minutes of the third period. Unfortunately, the game was played on a night when the temperature hovered around twenty-five below zero and only a handful of spectators turned up at the rink.

"There was no great fuss about the seven goals at the time," said Malone. "It was only a night's work as far as I was concerned. The only thing I remember about it is that it was very cold outside."

The NHL's first playoff pitted Toronto against the Canadiens. The playoffs, a two-game total goals series, opened in Toronto on March 11, 1918.

The first game could have been mistaken for a barroom brawl. Bert Corbeau and Newsy Lalonde, of the Canadiens, seemed more intent on decapitating the Queen City boys than on scoring. Toronto accumulated seven goals, as opposed to three for the Canadiens, sending the series back to Montreal. Home ice had no sedative effect on the Canadiens. Lalonde knocked Harry Meeking unconscious with a brutal blow, and Ken Randall was badly sliced by the sticks of Joe Hall and Lalonde. The intimidating tactics worked only to the extent that Montreal outscored Toronto 4-3, but Toronto won the series ten goals to seven.

Thus Toronto met Vancouver in the Stanley Cup finals, which opened in the Queen City on March 20, 1918. This time it was to be a best-of-five series, and it went the limit. Toronto won the first and third games; Vancouver won the second and fourth.

The fifth and final match, played on March 30, was the best of the series. Fred "Cyclone" Taylor, the kid from Listowel, scored the first goal in the first period, and ace goalie Hugh Lehman appeared capable of providing Vancouver with a shutout. But Alf Skinner tied the score, setting the stage for substitute Corbett Denneny to score the winner.

Toronto's triumph was not the forerunner of a dynasty. A year later the Canadiens emerged as the dominant team, finishing first as a prelude to a Stanley Cup meeting with the Metropolitans in Seattle. It proved to be a memorable series in an entirely negative way.

A worldwide influenza epidemic had spread to the Pacific Coast and almost caused the Cup finals to be cancelled before they even began. It was eventually to be known as the "Unfinished Series." Late in the fourth game Joe Hall, who nearly collapsed on the ice, was rushed to a hospital.

Immediately after the game several other Canadiens, including Lalonde and manager George Kennedy, were bedded with influenza but none as bad as Joe Hall. The belief was that the Montreal players had contracted the disease while sightseeing in Victoria, British Co-lumbia, but this was never ascertained.

With the series tied at two apiece an attempt was made to finish the play-off for the Stanley Cup. Kennedy requested permission to "borrow" players from Victoria to finish the series, but the hosts declined the bid and the play-off was canceled without a winner.

Six days after he had stumbled off the ice, Joe Hall died of influenza in a Seattle hospital. His friend and admirer, Joe Malone, was the most seriously affected by the news because he believed that Hall never had the opportunity to erase the bad name he had acquired. "There were plenty of huge, rough characters on the ice in Joe's time," said Joe Malone, "and he was able to stay in there with them for more than eighteen years. His death was a tragic and shocking climax to one of the most surprising of all Stanley Cup series."

In some ways the 1918-19 season proved a line of demarcation for the fledgling NHL. Play resumed the following autumn and hockey's major league entered the new decade with a distillation of anxiety and exuberance. Within five years it would become a major force on the international scene and set the stage for an amazing spread of the game in the United States.

CHAPTER THREE
The Booming Twenties

THE NEW DECADE BEGAN with a modicum of uncertainty at both ends of the Canadian professional hockey spectrum. In the East, Quebec's franchise foundered to the point that it was moved to Hamilton for the 1920-21 season and the "new" Tigers competed with Ottawa, Toronto and the Canadiens in a four-team National Hockey League. Out West, the Patrick brothers' Pacific Coast Hockey Association embraced Vancouver, Seattle and Victoria.

Nobody was quite sure how fast big-time hockey would grow but there continued to be encouraging signs, particularly in the 1921 Stanley Cup finals between Ottawa and Vancouver. The five-game series, held at Denman Street Arena in Vancouver, was a smash hit at the gate. Game One drew 11,000 spectators, which immediately made it the world's biggest hockey crowd.

The game, on April 4, 1921, inspired such interest that more than 2,000 fans were left standing outside the arena for lack of seats. In all more than 50,000 paying customers went through the turnstiles during the five-game set, a testimony to the ice game's popularity.

On the artistic side, Ottawa prevailed for the second straight year thanks to a pair of goals by Jack Darragh after Alf Skinner had staked the home team to a 1-0 lead. The Senators thus had the distinction of becoming the first NHL club to win back-to-back Stanley Cups.

Yet another signal for hockey's boom was evident in the autumn of 1921 when a competitor for both the NHL and PCHA was born on Canada's prairies. A four-team — Regina, Saskatoon, Calgary, Edmonton — Western Canada Hockey League launched its maiden season in 1921-22 and was considered powerful enough to induce the PCHA to engage it in a playoff series. The winner would then challenge the NHL champion for The Stanley Cup.

Although the WCHL didn't top its older rival, it did manage to ice a reasonably competitive challenge via the Regina Capitals who beat Vancouver Millionaires, 2-1, in the open-

Nobody contributed more to hockey's growth than Lester Patrick. Nicknamed the "Silver Fox," Patrick became manager and coach of the New York Rangers when they entered the NHL in 1926-27. Although he never played a skating position with his club, Lester worked out with them frequently.

ing match of the two-game, total goal series. In the end Vancouver prevailed with a 4-0 edge in Game Two and an overall count of 5-2. That set the stage for a Stanley Cup final between Vancouver and Toronto whose team was renamed the St.Patrick's from its previous handle, the Arenas.

The five-game series, which was played in Toronto, swung back and forth starting with a 4-3 Millionaires' win but in the end Cecil "Babe" Dye of the St.Patrick's scored four goals in the decisive fifth game to provide Toronto with a 5-1 win and The Stanley Cup.

Dye, who was a professional baseball player in the summer, epitomized the rise of the superstar in hockey. As more leagues and

teams sprouted, so, too, did interest in particular players. In the East, for example, a majestic French-Canadian goaltender named Georges Vezina captured the imagination of Montreal Canadiens fans with his acrobatic performances and was nicknamed "The Chicoutimi Cucumber" because of his cool play and, of course, the city of his birth.

During the 1923-24 season Vezina allowed only 48 goals in 24 games, including three shutouts for a goals against average of 2.00. He then blanked Ottawa, 1-0, in the first game of the playoffs and sparkled as the Canadiens swept the series 4-2.

In the Stanley Cup finals, Vezina was obliged to face not one but two challengers — the Calgary Tigers and Vancouver Maroons (formerly the Millionaires). This curious state-of-affairs developed because of a dispute between the WCHL and PCHA which resulted in both teams arriving in Montreal to take on Les Canadiens.

With Vezina in complete control, the Habs eliminated Vancouver by scores of 3-2 and 2-1 and then shellacked Calgary 6-1 and 3-0. (Incidentally, poor ice conditions in Montreal necessitated a change of venue for the final game which was held in Ottawa. Including the two

NHL playoff contests, Vezina had played in a total of six championship games and allowed only six goals for a remarkable 1.00 goals against average.

Nobody knew it at the time but the stage gradually was being set for a traumatic upheaval in hockey's balance of power. It began with the decline and fall of the PCHA. Seattle's

Left: The Edmonton Eskimos, with stars such as "Duke" Keats (top row, third from right) and Ty Arbour (top row, second from right) were no match for the Ottawa Senators in the 1922-23 Stanley Cup final. (Photo courtesy of the Alberta Provincial Archives).

Below: One of the earliest NHL scoring aces was Nels Stewart, alias "Ole' Poison." Stewart's best years were with the Montreal Maroons, who shared Montreal's fandom with the Canadiens.

Above: The first team to represent the New York area was the Americans (1925), formerly the Hamilton Tigers. Their goaltender, Roy ("Shrimp") Worters eventually made it into the Hockey Hall of Fame.

Opposite: The first American team to enter the NHL was the Boston Bruins in 1924. In 1928 they won their first Stanley Cup. Their stars included Eddie Shore (top row, far left), the NHL's best defenseman, and Aubrey ("Dit") Clapper (top row, second from right), a crack forward.

once-proud franchise was eliminated when its home rink was razed to be replaced by a garage of all things. Without the Metropolitans, Frank and Lester Patrick realized that they couldn't operate with a two-team (Victoria and Vancouver) league so they did the next best thing and merged with four-team Western Canada League, about to embark on its fourth season.

Thus, the WCHL opened the 1924-25 campaign with the two additions from the Pacific as well as Calgary, Regina, Saskatoon, and Edmonton. This was well and good for the moment but bigger things were happening in bigger places.

A huge, new Madison Square Garden was under construction in New York City and Manhattan promoters began eyeing a major league hockey franchise. Likewise, entrepreneurs in other U.S. centers such as Boston and Pittsburgh also were making inquiries.

New England grocery magnate Charles F. Adams ventured to Montreal for the 1924 Stanley Cup finals and was smitten by the spectacle. "When he returned home," his son Weston related, "he told us this was the greatest hockey he had ever seen. He wouldn't be happy until he had a franchise."

Adams' wish was granted when in 1924

Right: Doctors feared that Mervyn Dutton would never play hockey again following a life-threatening injury in WWI. But the redheaded speedster not only returned to pro hockey, he became the leader of one of the NHL's most colourful teams in the Twenties, the New York Americans.

the NHL governors voted to grant him the first American franchise. During his Canadian travels, Adams met a crusty, dour Scot by the name of Art Ross, who had once enjoyed a successful playing career, and named him coach, general manager and scout of the new team, the Boston Bruins.

Even then, expansion teams suffered. The Bruins finished the 1924-25 season with an awful record of six wins and twenty-four losses, lagging far behind another recent entry, the Montreal Maroons, not to mention the Canadiens, Toronto, and Hamilton.

At the mid-point of the Twenties, two professional leagues dominated. The Western Canada Hockey League featured Calgary, Saskatoon,

Victoria, Edmonton, Vancouver and Regina while the NHL also was a six-team loop including the two Montreal clubs, Canadiens and Maroons.

Although the NHL was the wealthier of the two, the WCHL also was formidable in terms of talent. Future Hall of Famers such as Bill Cook, Dick Irvin, Duke Keats, Red Dutton and Bullet Joe Simpson were among the western aces. And if anything confirmed the high level

Four stars from the booming Twenties: (Clockwise from top left) Frank "King" Clancy, Sylvio Mantha, Frank Boucher, and Howie Morenz.

Clancy was acquired by the Maple Leafs soon after they changed their name from the St. Patricks. Team owner Conn Smythe had to first win a bet at the racetrack to afford the colourful defenseman.

Sylvio Mantha was a matinee idol with the Canadiens — the most romanticized team of the 1920s.

Frank Boucher — once a member of the Royal Canadian Mounted Police — signed with the original New York Rangers in 1926. He centered the legendary line flanked by right wing Bill Cook and left wing Bun Cook. Boucher won the Lady Byng Trophy so many times that Lady Byng herself gave him the silverware to keep and had a new trophy struck for other players.

Morenz popularized the speed and thrills of pro hockey. Variously dubbed the "Mitchell Meteor" and the "Stanford Streak, Morenz became the darling of American fans, resulting in franchises in New York, Chicago, and Detroit.

Right: If a photo can be called a hoax, this is it. The Rangers attempted to capitalize on the publicity created by general manager Lester Patrick playing goalie as an emergency substitute during the 1928 playoffs. Without actual photos of Patrick, a composite picture was created in which Patrick's head was affixed to the body of Lorne Chabot.

Opposite page: the toughest player of a tough era, Eddie Shore was also one of the most popular. Those who saw him in his prime suggest that Shore was among the meanest, most physically aggressive players the NHL has ever known.

of WCHL play it was the performance of Lester Patrick's Victoria Cougars in the Stanley Cup finals against the Canadiens. The westerners routed Montreal three games to one and for the last time the WCHL basked in championship glory. A year later Victoria again went to the finals but lost the Cup three games to one.

The series marked the last time a representative other than an NHL club participated in the Stanley Cup playoffs. Time — and finances — simply had run out on the WCHL.

Economics militated again smaller cities such as Saskatoon and Edmonton particularly since the clamor for hockey players was becoming more intense in the United States. A year after the Bruins became NHL members, the Hamilton Tigers were purchased by a New York group and moved to the new Madison Square Garden where they were renamed the Americans.

Meanwhile, the WCHL moguls conceded that they no longer could sustain their losses but also wanted some value for their players. As a result there were wholesale purchases of stickhandlers by representatives of new franchises in Chicago, Detroit and New York; this time with a club called the Rangers. The WCHL, which closed after the 1925-26 season, ultimately proved the prime feeder for the expanding NHL which became a ten-team league split between Canadian and American divisions. Ottawa, Montreal Canadiens, New York Americans, Montreal Maroons and Toronto embraced the Canadian side while the Rangers, Chicago Blackhawks, Boston, Detroit Cougars and Pittsburgh Pirates were in the American Division.

Boston already had begun developing into a formidable squad under the aegis of Art Ross while the Americans, replete with a Broadway playboy image, managed to titillate New York fans with their dashing — if not always winning — style.

The infusion of WCHL talent gave the subsequent new NHL clubs instant credibility as well. Madison Square Garden owners originally hired Toronto hockey manager Conn Smythe to construct the brand new Rangers but when Smythe quarreled with the high command he was replaced before the 1926-27 season opened by Lester Patrick. The combination of Smythe and Patrick signees, including Bill and Bun Cook, Frank Boucher and Ching Johnson, provided the Broadway Blueshirts with a rare competitive edge among new teams.

With players acquired from the Portland Rosebuds, the Chicago Blackhawks finished a respectable third, right behind the Rangers in the American section's first season while the Detroit Cougars, who were stocked with Victoria stickhandlers, were at the bottom of the American Division.

Ottawa went on to win The Stanley Cup, defeating the Bruins who were becoming an American power. While it is true that the Rangers won The Cup in their second season of play, it was the Bostonians who really cut a quality niche. In 1927-28 they finished first, repeated in 1928-29 and won the Stanley Cup in 1929 with a three-straight sweep over the Canadiens in a best-of-five series.

Hockey caught fire in the states because of its blend of speed, skill and toughness. Eddie Shore, who previously had been dubbed "The Edmonton Express," became the darling of Beantown because of his robust hitting and dazzling end-to-end rushes.

New York fans were taken by the pinpoint passing of the Cook Brothers and the marvelous stickhandling exhibited by their center, Frank Boucher. Lester Patrick quickly established himself as the patriarch of the Gotham ice wars and something of a living legend after he put on the goalie pads at age 44 after his netminder Lorne Chabot was injured in the second game of the 1928 finals against the Maroons. Incredibly, Patrick stood the test and helped his club to a 2-1 overtime victory; one that was pivotal for the Rangers march to their first Stanley Cup.

There were problems to be sure on both sides of the border. The Pittsburgh club foundered on the ice and at the box office and the once-glorious Ottawa Senators also encountered money migraines. The Roarin' Twenties had come to a close and with the dawn of the 1930s, North America found itself gripped in the Great Depression. Hard times would be ahead for the two nations as well as the National Hockey League.

CHAPTER FOUR

Through the Depression

THE DECADE OF THE TWENTIES ENDED with NHL leaders doing exactly what they are doing today; seeking ways and means of making hockey a more palatable dish for the customers, while making a buck for themselves.

Nowadays, the accent is on television. At the start of the 1929-30 season, when radio was in its infancy, the ice lords concentrated on the product on the ice. Their conclusion was that the game had been too low-scoring and not fast enough.

The solution was to divide the ice into three separate zones which were designated defensive, offensive and neutral. Forward passing would be allowed in each of the three zones but passing from one player to another in a different zone would be forbidden.

Again, like today, the owners felt obliged to cater to an American audience that seemed bent on more action and higher scoring games. Whether the rules would work or not was another story but the early returns were positive. Where a year earlier Irvine "Ace" Bailey led the NHL in scoring with 22 goals and 32 points,

under the revised rules, Ralph "Cooney" Weiland of Boston became the new scoring leader having tallied a then remarkable 43 goals and 30 assists in 44 games.

To accommodate the new fans, larger arenas began sprouting throughout the league. Madison Square Garden was the first of the big indoor sports palaces to be erected but it soon was followed by Chicago Stadium, Boston Garden, Olympia Stadium in Detroit and Toronto's Maple Leaf Gardens.

This made it difficult for cities with smaller seating capacities, which explains, in part, why teams failed in Pittsburgh and Philadelphia. The Pirates were moved to the City of Brotherly Love in time for the 1930-31 season and were renamed the Quakers. The new club sorely lacked talent and could easily qualify on the list of all-time worst teams. The Quakers finished the campaign with a record of only four wins, 36 losses and four ties. They passed out of existence before the 1931-32 season began.

An offshoot of the new offensive thrust was the emergence of powerful forward lines which were — each in their own distinctive way — exceptionally colorful. The Bruins boasted a trio comprised of Cooney Weiland, Dutch Gainor and Dit Clapper which was dubbed The Dynamite Line. The boisterous Toronto Maple Leafs, who were called the "Gashouse Gang", developed a splendid triumvirate. Their center was "Gentleman Joe" Primeau who flanked Harvey "Busher" Jackson on the left and Charlie Conacher on the right. Youthfully exuberant, the three naturally were dubbed the "Kid Line."

Not to be outdone, the Montreal Maroons offered the "S" Line led by Nels "Ole Poison" Stewart, Babe Siebert and Reg Smith. The cross town rival Canadiens featured fleet Howie "The Stratford Flash" Morenz centering Johnny "Black Cat" Gagnon and Aurel Joliat. Arguably, the most effective unit of all — and for the longest time — was the New York Rangers pairing of the Cook Brothers, Bill and Bun, with Frank Boucher at center.

With the continent in the midst of The Great Depression, the NHL provided lively entertainment and no team created a more favorable impression than Les Canadiens, otherwise known as the "Flying Frenchmen," or the "Habitants (Habs)."

Winners of the 1931 Stanley Cup, the Habs took aim at another championship with the Gagnon-Morenz-Joliat line leading the way.

Below: A sure sign of early NHL hockey was the cap-wearing goaltender. Here Andy Aitkenhead of the New York Rangers makes a save against the Detroit Red Wings. On the far right is the legendary Rangers defenseman Ivan "Ching" Johnson.

Herb Lewis of the Detroit Red Wings says: "I go for Camels in a big way!"

THE lightning-quick camera eye caught *Herb Lewis* (*above, left*) in this slashing set-to before the goal. Next split-second he scored! After the game (*right*), Herb said: "You bet I enjoy eating. And I'll give Camels credit for helping me enjoy my food. Smoking Camels with my meals and afterwards eases tension. Camels set me right!"

Camel smokers enjoy smoking to the full. It's Camels for a "lift." It's Camels again "for digestion's sake." Thanks to Camel's aid, the flow of the important digestive fluids —*alkaline* digestive fluids—speeds up. A sense of well-being follows. So make it Camels—the live-long day.

Above: Hockey became so popular in the 1930s that major cigarette companies, such as Camel, employed stars like Herb Lewis of the Red Wings to promote their brands. Here is a typical magazine ad from that era.

Right: Another form of promotion was the beer company commercial. Here, New York Rangers (left to right) Muzz Patrick, Mac Colville, and Dave Kerr churn up the ice for a photo used by Rheingold Beer in a "Twist it open/ Twist it closed" ad campaign.

fter a first place finish, Montreal eliminated oston in a pulsating series and then met the lackhawks. Well-coached by former player 'ick Irvin, the Hawks took a 2-1 lead in games nd a 2-0 lead in what could have been the urth and Cup-winning game for them. But agnon rallied Montreal with two goals and it Lepine followed with two more as Les anadiens prevailed, 4-2. The finale was a clas- c example of a tight-checking game being a riller. One break would mean the game and fontreal got that break when Gagnon broke ne deadlock and Morenz delivered the insur- nce goal for the Canadiens second straight up.

Until that time no team ever had won three traight NHL championships but the Habs ap- eared capable of such a feat. They finished rst in the 1931-32 season but never completed their mission. Inspired by Conn Smythe — the same chap who originally designed the Rang- ers in 1926 — the Maple Leafs celebrated com- pletion of their new home on November 12, 1931 with a vibrant distillation of brashness and clever play. Captivating players such as Reginald "Red" Horner, Clarence "Hap" Day and Frank "King" Clancy spearheaded the Ma- ple Leafs (formerly the Toronto St.Patricks un- til Smythe changed the name) to playoff victo- ries over Chicago, the Maroons and, finally, the Rangers who were beaten in what was kid- dingly called the "Tennis Series" because of the final scores — 6-4, 6-2, 6-4. No club ever before had taken three consecutive matches to annex the Stanley Cup.

The Rangers defeat did not obscure the fact that they, along with Detroit, Boston and Montreal, all were hockey powers. In New York,

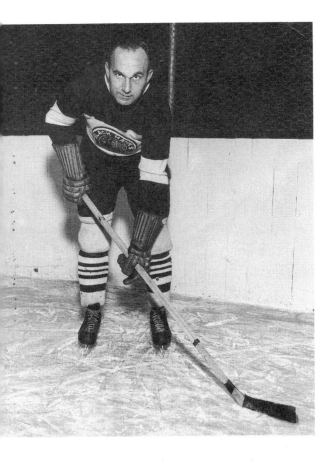

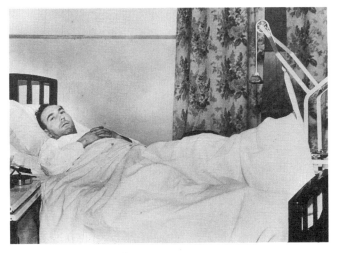

The saga of Howie Morenz is one of the most tragic in hockey annals. He was traded from the Montreal Canadiens to the Chicago Blackhawks in 1935 and then to the Rangers in the following season before returning to Montreal in 1936-37. Having regained his flair, Morenz suffered a broken leg against the Blackhawks in 1937. Hospitalized, he took a sudden and inexplicable turn for the worse and died March 8, 1937.

Above: Goalie Earl Robertson (previously with Edmonton) makes a big save for the N.Y. Americans with the aid of Lorne Carr. Most unusual is the helmeted Bruin at the left. Normally, the only players to wear helmets at the professional level were those recovering from injury.

the constant battling between the Americans and Rangers produced one of the keenest intra-city rivalries the NHL has known although the competition in Montreal between the Canadiens and Maroons was equally intense.

For Manhattanites, the Rangers emerged

as the blue-bloods of hockey because they had the backing of wealthy Madison Square Garden when the "Amerks," as the Americans were known, had been bankrolled by a bootlegger named "Big Bill" Dwyer whose fortunes ebbed with the end of Prohibition. Thus, the Americans, who unlike the Rangers had to pay a steep rental fee to the Garden, limped along as the poor cousin to the Rangers, who still boasted such glamorous players as the Cook Brothers, Frank Boucher, Cecil Dillon, Ott Heller and Murray Murdoch.

Under Lester Patrick's tutelage, the Cook-Boucher combine collaborated for one last tanley Cup in 1933 when they beat the Maple Leafs three games to one in a best-of-five game eries. Bill Cook's last hurrah in the Cup finals vas the winning goal in overtime of Game 'our. Cecil Dillon was the goal-scoring hero vith a total of eight for the entire playoffs.

The Great Depression continued to take its oll on the continent in general and the NHL in articular but all nine franchises (Toronto, Canadiens, Maroons, Ottawa, Americans, Chiago, Rangers, Detroit and Boston) returned or the 1933-34 season although the Detroiters vent into receivership and were rescued by Canadian grain magnate James Norris, Sr.

As has been the case since the game's ineption, hockey continued to refine its rules and accoutrements. For the new campaign, the NHL ordered that "visible timing devices be displayed at all rinks" and that "not more than hree players, including the goalkeeper of the defending side, may stand in the defending zone." Frank Patrick, who along with brother Lester, once had devised innovative rules for their Pacific Coast League, now was being creative for the NHL and persuaded the owners to revise the officiating system so that there be two referees instead of a referee and a linesman.

The 1933-34 season was marked with triumph heavily tainted by tragedy. One of the more traumatic episodes involved popular Toronto forward Ace Bailey who was charged from behind by Boston's Eddie Shore. The collision sent Bailey to the hospital where he was feared dead. A pair of brain operations ultimately saved his life but Bailey never was able to play hockey again. Shore was suspended but later reinstated by league President Frank Calder.

A positive outgrowth of the incident was

Left: A traditional stock photo from the 1930's featured a team's defense line-up with a collectively intense look about it. This Rangers quintet does it well. Left to right: Earl Siebert, Doug Brennan, Ching Johnson, Jean Pusie, and Ott Heller.

Action in the Thirties!
*Don't let the black & white fool you —
hockey was as fast and wild then as it is
now, as these three classic shots illustrate.*

*Left: The most famous goalie with the
Toronto Maple Leafs was Walter "Turk"
Broda, who broke in with the team in
1936 and remained with them through
1951. Here, Broda deflects a Ranger shot
into the corner.*

*Right: Two Hall-of-Famers
lead the attack for the
Maple Leafs against the
Rangers. Joe Primeau, one
of the top stickhandlers of
the 1930s, moves over the
New York blueline while
defenseman Frank "King"
Clancy (right) jumps into
the rush.*

*Left: Ebenezer Goodfellow
(11) preceded Gordie Howe as
the ultimate Detroit hockey
hero. In this instance "Ebby's"
shot is blocked by Rangers
goalie Dave Kerr.*

Left: Among the most prominent families in hockey during the 1930s was the Patrick clan of New York. Lester (center) managed and coached the club, while sons Lynn, a left winger (left) and Muzz, a defenseman (right) starred for the Broadway Blueshirts.

the decision to hold an All-Star Game to benefit Bailey and his family. The event took place on February 10, 1934 at Toronto's Maple Leaf Gardens and would be the forerunner of future All-Star Games, which would be launched on a more formal scale after World War II.

Yet another tragedy would unfold in the playoffs when Blackhawks goalie Charlie Gardiner began suffering the effects of a chronic tonsil infection which, in turn, was causing uremic convulsions. Despite intense pain, Gardiner played through the series and backstopped Chicago to its first Stanley Cup with a 1-0 shutout over the Red Wings in what was to be his final game. Just two months later Gardiner died.

Prior to the 1934-35 season the Depression claimed Ottawa's proud hockey club. Because of red ink, the Senators packed their gear and moved to St.Louis and were renamed the Eagles. But one of the biggest stories of the year was the Canadiens decision to ship their erstwhile superstar Howie Morenz to the Blackhawks.

At the time the Habs were losing Montreal bragging rights to their Forum co-tenants, the Maroons, who represented the English-speaking population while the Canadiens carried the Gallic torch.

Although the Maroons finished second in the Canadian Division behind Toronto (but nine points ahead of the Habs), they nevertheless remained a power to be reckoned with in the playoffs because of Alex Connell's superlative goaltending. Montreal beat the defending champion Blackhawks in the opening round and then swept the Maple Leafs in three straight games with enormous help from Connell and such goal-scorers as Dave Trottier, Cy Wentworth and Baldy Northcott.

A year later the Maroons were involved in another historic event; the longest NHL game ever played. The marathon took place on March 24, 1936 at The Forum in the opening contest of the preliminary playoff between Montreal and Detroit. A 0-0 tie prevailed until what amounted to the ninth period of play. Modere "Mud" Bruneteau, who had been a bench-warmer for most of the game, scored the winning goal for the Red Wings after 116 minutes and 30 seconds of overtime. Hours later, Bruneteau visited the downcast losing goalie Lorne Chabot to extend his condolences.

The victory gave impetus to a three-game sweep by Detroit and sent them winging to the Motor City's first Stanley Cup celebration. In the final round, the Red Wings eliminated Toronto three games to one and coach Jack "Jolly Jawn" Adams became established as one of the premier coaches in the game.

By this time St.Louis had expired (prior to the 1935-36 season) and the NHL was reduced to an eight-team league though still troubled with fiscal woes. Both the Americans and Ma-

Below: Over the years the Chicago Blackhawks wore the most colourful uniforms. Their black, red and white striped outfits from the 1938-39 season were among the best. Here, goalie Mike Karakas foils a bid by Eddie Wiseman (no. 10) of the New York Americans at Chicago Stadium.

roons struggled to stay afloat but both remained league members in 1936-37, a season most notable because of Detroit's second straight Stanley Cup championship.

It also was a year that, sorrowfully to many fans, featured a changing of the guard. The Rangers long-acclaimed line of Bill and Bun Cook with Frank Boucher had reached the end of its trail and, similarly, Toronto's Kid Line of Joe Primeau, Busher Jackson and Charlie Conacher also had faded to virtual insignificance.

Others who starred in the NHL's first booming decade also were encountering difficulties and, in some cases, tragedy. Howie Morenz, who had been the darling of Montreal until the Canadiens traded him to Chicago finally returned to the Habs in 1936-37 and was skating up a storm until he suffered a badly broken leg during a game. Although his hospitalization seemed routine enough, Morenz suffered a nervous breakdown during his sabbatical and died on March 8, 1937.

*Stars on the move: The New York Americans liked to sign hockey immortals in the twilight of their careers.
Two examples are ex-Bruin Eddie Shore (top shots, left and right), shown first in a Boston uniform and then with his
new jersey, and like wise with ex-Ranger Ching Johnson (bottom shots).*

Above: "Gentleman Joe" Primeau was the ace center for Toronto's "Kid Line", with Busher Jackson and Charlie Conacher.

right time and in the finals against Toront(even managed to win despite the loss of regu lar goalie Mike Karakas who had suffered broken toe in the previous series.

Prior to Game One, the Blackhawks high command searched the city of Toronto for replacement netminder and finally found on(in a pub. His name was Alfie Moore and he had been a rather obscure pro. But he quickly signe(an NHL contract and played well enough against the Maple Leafs to come away with a 3 1 win. Karakas eventually returned to the lineu[and spearheaded the Chicagoans to a three games-to-one upset over the favored Leafs. I was Chicago's second Stanley Cup champion ship.

Fiscal problems continued to dog the Ma roons and Americans. The Amerks, with Red Dutton in command, managed to stay afloa

As the old warriors departed, fresh new faces caught the fans' attention. The Boston Bruins introduced a trio from the Kitchener, Ontario that included Milt Schmidt at center with Bobby Bauer on right wing and Woody Dumart on the left. Dubbed the "Kraut Line," the unit helped Boston to the best record of the 1937-38 season. Meanwhile, the Toronto Maple Leafs were infused with vibrant youngsters including former 1936 Olympian Syl Apps, a brilliant center from Paris, Ontario and Gordie Drillon, a husky right wing with a devastating shot. In goal the Maple Leafs were protected by Walter "Turk" Broda who, in time, would become one of hockey's best clutch performers.

The 1937-38 season was anomalous in one respect and that was logic. Although the Bruins finished with a top-heavy 30-11-7 record, they never made it to the Stanley Cup finals. Instead, the cherished Cup was won by a team with a regular season record of 14-25-9. Incredibly, the Chicago Blackhawks got hot at the

bove and left: The 1930s closed with the emergence of
et another great young goaltender. Dubbed "Mister
ero," Frankie Brimsek went from Eveleth, Minnesota
o the Boston Bruins, where he established himself as
ne of the greatest goalies of all time.

nd even enjoyed a brief artistic revival. Dutton
hrewdly obtained older aces such as the Rang-
rs' popular defenseman Ching Johnson and
Hooley Smith, who had starred for the Ma-
oons. The Americans' last heroic achievement
vas knocking the Rangers out of the 1938
layoffs in a stirring series that went the limit.

The Amerks lasted into the 1938-39 cam-
aign but the Maroons folded, thus cutting the

NHL down to only seven teams and one division. Still, the hockey was good and new heroes emerged. One of the least likely of them
was Mel Hill, a third-string Bruins forward
who had played in the shadow of the Kraut
Liners, Bill Cowley and Dit Clapper.

Hill suddenly became a headliner in the
playoffs when he discovered the knack of scoring overtime goals. In the thrilling seven-game
Boston-Rangers series, Hill was the overtime
winner in Games One and Two. But the best was
yet to come. After the playoff reached the decisive seventh game and eventually went into
triple overtime, Hill delivered the winning goal.
Thus, his new sobriquet, "Sudden Death Hill."

Fortified with Hill and the impregnable goaltending of Frank Brimsek — earlier nicknamed "Mister Zero" after he posted ten shutouts in 1938-39 — the Bruins overwhelmed Toronto four games to one in the Stanley Cup finals. If ever a dynasty loomed on the NHL horizon as the 1930s peeled off to a close, it was the Boston sextet.

In addition to Brimsek and the Krauts, Boston offered a varied display of talent including Roy Conacher, kid brother of Charlie and a sharpshooter in his own right, Bill "Flash" Hollett, one of the few offensive-minded defensemen of the era and the magical Bill Cowley, whose stickhandling has seen few equals in league history.

But Boston's quest for another Stanley Cup would be detoured by two disparate events the emergence of the New York Rangers as a league power and the outbreak of World War II, which would decimate the rosters of most NHL clubs.

Right: One of the most underrated defensemen of all time, Art Coulter, captained the Rangers' Stanley cup winning team in 1939-40. After the U.S. entered WWII, Coulter joined the U.S. Coast Guard and played for their team, the Cutters, based at Curtis Bay in Maryland.

CHAPTER FIVE

The War Years and Beyond

TWO MONTHS BEFORE THE FIRST GAME of the 1939-40 season the guns of September roared across the Polish frontier. Nazi armored columns blitzed their way toward Warsaw and, almost overnight, the British Commonwealth, (including, of course, Canada) found itself at war with Hitler's Germany.

When the Detroit Red Wings opened the new season on November 2, 1939 at Chicago Stadium, the effects of wartime on the NHL were negligible but that would change in the months to come. In the meantime, hockey fans concentrated on the new season and a remarkably tight race between four solid teams, the Bruins, Rangers, Maple Leafs and Blackhawks.

Boston had the best balance, with Frankie Brimsek continuing to excel in goal, fronted by a well-balanced defense and two mighty forward lines, the Krauts (Schmidt-Dumart-Bauer) and a second unit comprised of Eddie Wiseman, Roy Conacher and Bill Cowley.

The Bruins finished first, three points ahead of the Rangers and scored 170 goals, 34 more than the runner-up New Yorkers. But the

Blackhawks and Red Wings had much to commend. Detroit developed a budding superstar in Syd Howe (no relation to Gordie who would become a Red Wing many years later) while the Blackhawks had such redoubtables as Cully Dahlstrom, Mush March, Bill Carse and Johnny Gottselig.

Montreal's season virtually ended before it could get started when popular defenseman Babe Siebert drowned before training camp opened. A second benefit All-Star Game for a Canadien — the first was for Howie Morenz — was held on October 29, 1939 at The Forum. Proceeds of the exhibition went to the Siebert Family.

The Canadiens never could get untracked and finished seventh and last (10-33-5), nine points behind the sixth place New York Americans. In those days all a club had to do in order to qualify for a playoff berth was finish sixth or higher, which the Amerks managed to do. Despite their lowly (15-29-4), state, the Americans unearthed a major talent in Tommy "Cowboy" Anderson, a left wing obtained from Detroit

Above: The goal that capped the greatest comeback in Stanley Cup history. After trailing the Red Wings three games to none in the 1942 Stanley Cup finals, the Maple Leafs won the next four games straight. Pete Langelle (8) has just fired what proved to be the winning goal in the seventh game of this incredible series.

who would become one of the NHL's foremost scoring threats.

From the season's start, the Rangers and Bruins engaged in a neck-and-neck race for first place. The Broadway Blueshirts had undergone a significant pre-season change at the helm when their perennial coach and manager, Lester Patrick, abdicated his bench job to con-

centrate solely on front office work. Patrick' longtime center, Frank Boucher, who had on of hockey's keenest minds, took over the coach ing and promptly created an awesome squa from goalie Davey Kerr to defenseman Ot Heller on out to exceptional forwards Brya Hextall, Lynn Patrick (Lester's son), Phi Watson, Alex Shibicky and the Colville Broth ers, Mac and Neil.

"We had great respect for what the Bruin had done," said Boucher, "but we also believe that we had reached a level where we coul challenge them for the Cup."

In one respect, the Bruins' power was di minished when Eddie Shore — after squab bling with management over his right to shut

Left:The decade's dominant coach — a former star defenseman for the Maple Leafs, Clarence "Hap" Day succeeded Dick Irvin as Toronto coach and led the Leafs to Cup wins in 1942, 1945, 1947, 1948, and 1949.

Below: The 1942 finals erupted in a classic melee after game four when Red Wings manager Jack Adams (wearing hat to the left of no. 11) punched referee Mel Harwood (obscured by Adams). The players are Eddie Wares of the Wings (11) and Wally Stanowski of the Maple Leafs. Adams was suspended for the duration of the series. Toronto won the next three games.

Rejected by the Maple Leafs, Bill Durnan was signed by Montreal in 1943 and instantly became the NHL's premier goalie, not to mention the only ambidextrous goaltender in the NHL. He won the Vezina Trophy in 1944, 1945, 1946, 1947, 1949 and 1950. He's seen above stopping Buddy O'Connor (5) of the Rangers.

tle between Boston and his newly-acquired Springfield American League franchise — was dealt to the Americans. But the Hub sextet was so strong that not even Shore's absence could prevent their relentless march to first place.

However, the playoffs were another story. As often is the case, a hot goaltender will decide a short series and in this case the Rangers had a sizzling Davey Kerr who produced no less than three shutouts in six games against Mister Zero Brimsek and the Bruins. With Boston out of the way, the New Yorkers' obstacle was the Maple Leafs. The finals went to six games and was settled in sudden death overtime on Bryan Hextall's shot past Turk Broda. at Maple Leaf Gardens.

Dick Irvin, who had been coaching Toronto for years, accepted an invitation to move to Montreal for the following season where he would take over a decrepit Canadiens' club and shape them up for years to come. The Maple Leafs replaced Irvin with a former stalwart defenseman, Clarence "Hap" Day, who only recently had become a referee.

Once again a four-team race developed for first place with Boston still holding the edge and Toronto, Detroit and the Rangers following in that order. The Blackhawks, who were having goaltending problems, tried a young American-born puck stopper named Sam LoPresti who proved more courageous than terribly capable.

Playing the Bruins at Boston Garden one night, LoPresti was assaulted with an NHL record 83 shots and gave up only three goals in a 3-2 defeat. In time LoPresti would become a U.S. Navy seaman whose ship was torpedoed in the Atlantic. Adrift for weeks, LoPresti finally was rescued near the coast of Africa and lived to tell his incredible tale.

Goaltending on virtually every team was at a qualitative peak during the 1940-41 season. Frankie Brimsek had a league-leading six shutouts but Turk Broda led all of his peers with a 2.06 goals against average. Claude "Bonnie Prince Charlie" Rayner of the Americans and Johnny Mowers of Detroit represented the new guard among the padded warriors, each displaying superior talents almost from the very first save.

Innovation was the order of the day. The Blackhawks' coach Paul Thompson shocked crowds by pulling his goaltender and replacing him with a forward during power play situations while Dick Irvin tried alternating his two goalies every seven minutes or so during the games.

Boston had the best idea of all; quality. At one point in the season the Bruins amassed a 23-game undefeated streak which enabled them to finish five points ahead of the second place Maple Leafs.

What better drama than a Boston-Toronto meeting in the opening playoff round; and what a series it was! The teams battled to a seventh game in which the lead seesawed back and forth. Bucko McDonald, known primarily for his bodychecking, staked Toronto to a 1-0 lead but Boston knotted the count when another defenseman, Flash Hollett tied the score. Mel "Sudden Death" Hill, a Bruin hero of yesteryear, settled matters with the third and final goal.

The Red Wings battled their way to the finals for the right to challenge Boston but it was no contest — 3-2, 2-1, 4-2, 3-1, all Bruins.

Under normal circumstances, the Bruins could have been expected to dominate the NHL for at least three or four years because of their talent surplus but these weren't ordinary times.

By November 1, 1941, when the Canadiens and Maple Leafs hosted the Red Wings and Rangers, respectively to unveil the new season, World War II had flared for two years in Europe and Asia. What had begun as a trickle of big-leaguers joining the armed forces — the Rangers defense star Murray Patrick was one of the first to enlist in the U.S. Army — turned

Left: The outbreak of WWII meant that many top NHL players joined the armed forces. The Chicago Blackhawks lost Sam LoPresti, who still holds the record for most saves in a game (80) by a goalie (March 4, 1941). LoPresti joined the U.S. Naval Armed Guard and went down in the Atlantic after his ship was torpedoed by the Nazis. Adrift for weeks, Sam was rescued off the coast of Africa.

into a torrent after Pearl Harbor Day (December 7, 1941) leaving NHL rosters in a somewhat altered state.

Boston lost its Kraut Line when Schmidt, Dumart and Bauer enlisted in the Royal Canadian Air Force while others followed suit. Among the first victims was Maple Leafs prospect Jack Fox and Rangers' potential star Dudley "Red" Garrett, both of whom were killed in action. In time nearly one hundred players will have worn the colors of the various Canadian and American armed forces.

One of the most unique of these units was the U.S. Coast Guard hockey team which was based at the Curtis Bay Yard in Baltimore, Maryland. Organized by Cliff MacLean, a former professional from the Michigan-Minnesota leagues, the Coast Guard sextet was comprised of mostly American-born players with an occasional Canadian — they had become naturalized American citizens — thrown in for good measure.

Art Coulter, captain of the Rangers Stanley Cup-winning team in 1940, and Frankie Brimsek were the biggest names on the Coast Guard Cutters but other NHLers graced the roster. These included Johnny Mariucci, a hard-nosed Blackhawks defenseman, and Bob "Killer" Dill, who played briefly for the Rangers. Top minor leaguers such as goalie Muzz Murray, defenseman Manny Cotlow and Mike Nardello also lent lustre to the Cutters who played in the Eastern League and won two Amateur Hockey Association of America senior championships. In addition, the Cutters frequently played — and beat — the best Canadian service squads.

Right: There were few more colourful characters in hockey than Defenseman Walter "Babe" Pratt, who starred for the Rangers' Stanley Cup winning squad in 1940 and scored the Cup-winning goal for the Maple Leafs in game seven of the 1945 finals against Detroit.

Having lost the Kraut Line, Boston slipped to third place in 1941-42 behind the Rangers and Toronto, although the margin was very slight. Chicago was a presentable fourth now that the Windy City boys had the swift and unpredictable brothers Max and Doug Bentley. The Canadiens rounded out the playoff qualifying teams in sixth place and the Americans, for the last time, brought up the rear.

A combination of insurmountable fiscal problems combined with a huge diminution of talent forced the Amerks to consider folding after the season. Several attempts had previously been made to resuscitate the franchise; the latest being a name-change, from New York Americans to Brooklyn Americans although the team still played out of the same Manhattan

BOSTON POST, FRIDAY, JANUARY 21, 1944

Fast Company! -:- -:- -:- By Bob Coyne

*Above: As this Boston Globe cartoon depicts, the Coast Guard Cutters included NHL stars Art Coulter (Rangers),
Frank Brimsek (Bruins) and Johnny Mauricci (Blackhawks). Amateur goalie Muzz Murray (Below)
got the thrill of his brief hockey career subbing for Brimsek with the Cutters.*

ddress as the Rangers. The theory behind the "Brooklyn" identity was to capitalize on the vehement Brooklyn Dodgers-New York Giants rivalry which captivated New York baseball fans at the time. Actually, the only thing Brooklyn about the Americans was the fact that manager Red Dutton relocated several of his players and their families to the Flatbush section of the Borough of Churches.

The first place finish was of no help to the Rangers once the playoffs began. New York

Left: Fighting has always been a part of hockey, even in the dying minutes of the Stanley Cup Finals. Here, Carl Liscombe of the Red Wings is being restrained by referee King Clancy, following his bout with Boston's Pat McCreary (down on the ice). McCreary may have lost this battle, but the Bruins won the war, completing a 3-1 victory and a four-game sweep of the Wings.

Below: Minor league hockey spawned more than fisticuffs like the bout pictured here. The white-sweatered referee is non other than millionare Harry Ornest who, through his hockey connections, went into vending machines, made a fortune, and in time owned the St. Louis Blues.

was wiped out of post-season play in the very first round by a hustling Toronto club which advanced to the finals where the Red Wings lay in wait.

To most observers, the result should not have been in doubt. Toronto had finished a fat fifteen points ahead of Detroit and had a formidable squad, orchestrated by Hap Day. Syl Apps, Gordie Drillon and Bob Davidson were among the more capable NHL scorers; the defense was experienced and stout while Turk Broda's goaltending always kicked up a notch when the chips were down.

But something went wrong right from the start. Detroit jumped all over their rivals from the opening period and employed a radical strategy conjured up by manager Jack Adams. Instead of entering the Toronto zone in the traditional manner of either stickhandling the puck or passing it from player to player, the Red Wings executed what was, for then, a revolutionary plan. When they approached the Maple Leafs blueliners, the Detroit players merely slipped the puck into the corner, did an end run around the defenders and then outraced them for the loose puck which promptly was put back into play with a deft pass.

Remarkably, the Red Wings won the firs three games, two of which had been played a Maple Leaf Gardens. Toronto was a city in a collective state of shock awaiting the final los at Detroit's Olympia Stadium. Hap Day scram bled for a way out of the morass and decided that severe measures were in order.

He benched top scorer Gordie Drillon, who had heretofore been a bust, as well as slow-footed defenseman Bucko McDonald. In their place he inserted an obscure forward, Don Metz, and a young defenseman named Ernie Dickens.

The Leafs responded just as Day had hoped and squeaked out a 4-3 win. Almost as eventful was the uprising at the final buzzer when Jack Adams, enraged at referee Mel Harwood's officiating, stormed at the official while detonating a near-riot on the ice. When the dust had cleared, Adams wound up being indefinitely suspended by NHL President Frank Calder. He was replaced behind the bench by aging forward Ebbie Goodfellow.

Meanwhile, Dickens and Don Metz (along with older brother Nick) played exceptionally well and the Leafs took Game Five, 9-3, to close to within a game of tying the series. They did just that in Game Six, thanks to Broda's airtight goaltending in a 3-0 win.

Until then no NHL club ever had lost the first three games of the Stanley Cup playoffs only to rebound and win the next four straight,

Below: Rare was the day when an entire forward line moved directly from the senior amateur ranks to the NHL. But it happened in 1945 when the New York Rangers promoted (left to right) Rene Trudell, Cal Gardner, and Church Russell from their New York Rovers farm team to the bigs. It happened shortly after the U.S. dropped an atomic bomb on Hiroshima. Not surprisingly, the unit was named the Atomic Line.

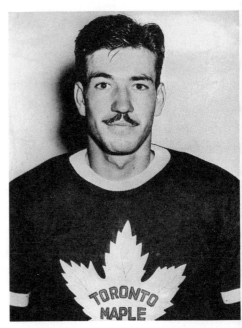

Leafs Triumphant!
One of the amazing stories of the immediate post-war years was Toronto boss Conn Smythe's rebuilding of the Maple Leafs into a dynasty. The team was built around goalie "Turk" Broda (above left) seen here stonewalling the Rangers. Other luminaries included mustachioed defenseman, Garth Boesch, and Captain Ted "Teeder" Kennedy, (right) planting one on the Stanley Cup in 1948.

but all bets were off before Game Seven at Maple Leaf Gardens. The largest crowd ever to see a hockey game in Canada (16,218) jammed the Gardens for the finale and they were treated to a doozie of a match.

Toronto trailed by a goal entering the final period unable to put the rubber past Johnny Mowers in the Red Wings net. The fiery Conn

Smythe, Toronto's leader who had enlisted in the Armed Forces, was permitted to take a leave in order to see his club perform in the finale. Smythe visited the dressing room after the second period and delivered a sermon that proved of enormous value. His Leafs took the ice and then proceeded to take the game away from Detroit. Veteran Sweeney Schriner scored a pair and Pete Langelle got the other, which was enough for the Maple Leafs to finish on top, 3-1.

The end of the season proved to be the last for the Americans. Although the NHL decided to subsidize the team, the league was unable to hammer out a deal with Madison Square Garden which seemed more intent on granting a New York hockey monopoly for its prime tenant, the Rangers. Thus, the Americans folded with a promise from the NHL that it could be revived after World War II.

A top priority among NHL leaders as they convened for their September 1942 meetings was whether or not the league could continue operations or if it would have to suspend play for the duration. Upon getting the green light from both the Canadian and American governments — baseball and football already had done

likewise — the NHL scheduled another season for 1942-43 aware that the calibre of play would be at an all-time low.

That, however, did not diminish fan enthusiasm. The war had signalled the end of the Great Depression and now people had more money in their pockets than in a decade. One of their favorite outlets was professional hockey and big crowds filled every NHL arena.

In response, the teams offered exciting if not particularly artistic fare. The Rangers, who lost more good players than any other club, predictably finished dead last while the other

Below: The Early All-Star games pitted the Stanley Cup champions against the All-Stars. In this 1948 match at Maple Leaf Gardens, action swirls around the Toronto net. Players are (left to right) Toronto defenseman Jim Thomson, Gordie Howe, "Wild Bill" Ezinicki, "Turk" Broda, and "Tough Tony" Leswick.

Above: One of the greatest goaltenders of all time, Jacques Plante, was the only goalie in history to knit his own wool toques. He is wearing one here as Herb Carnegie breaks in alone in a 1949-50 season Quebec Senior Hockey League game at the Montreal Forum. Carnegie was the playing for the Quebec Aces.

five clubs battled for the four remaining playoff berths. In the end, Chicago missed as well, winding up one point behind the fourth-place Canadiens.

To plug gaps created by enlistments, teams resorted to players who normally would have been considered too young or too old. The Bruins went to an extreme signing 16-year-old forward Armand (Bep) Guidolin while the Rangers, in a desperate attempt to locate a goalie — any goalie! — imported Steve Buzinski, who had played a low grade of senior hockey when he wasn't working full time. Steve was forced to play in front of a rather weak defense and wound up with the unfortunate nickname "Puckgoesinski."

One outcome of the personnel changes was an accent on scoring. Goalies and defensemen in many cases lacked the skills of those they replaced but the scorers were able to roam more easily. Chicago had two of the best in Doug and Max Bentley who finished first and third in scoring, respectively, around Boston's Bill Cowley. The Bentley's older brother, Reg, had a brief whirl with the Blackhawks playing on a line with Max and Doug. Unfortunately, Reg couldn't quite cut the big-league mustard and

soon left the NHL scene. Max, nicknamed The Dipsy Doodle Dandy From Delisle (Saskatchewan), won the Lady Byng Trophy.

Still another interesting character who emerged during the war was referee Bill Chadwick. An aspiring forward, Chadwick had lost the sight of his right eye following a hockey accident. Undaunted, he took up officiating and made it right to the top. His ultimate reward was inclusion in the Hockey Hall of Fame.

The rookie-of-the-year was Toronto forward Gaye Stewart who had played briefly in the 1942 Stanley Cup finals. A swift skater, Stewart was a principal in one of the season's most vicious fights during a Red Wings game. His opponent was Jimmy Orlando, a notorious battler. The two exchanged blows and then began hitting each other with their sticks before officials intervened. Both were fined $100 and suspended.

The traditional Detroit-Toronto rivalry extended into the playoffs only this time the Red Wings prevailed, winning the opening round in six games while Boston eliminated Montreal in five.

Unlike the 1942 version, the 1943 finals proved to be no contest. Detroit swept the Bruins in four games, 6-2, 4-3, 4-0, 2-0.

Having lost the Krauts and, more recently, Frankie Brimsek, the Bruins were in shambles by the next season, 1943-44, as they desperately tried to fill the huge goaltending void. By contrast, the Canadiens actually benefitted by the war because some players were able to obtain draft exemptions by working in defense plants. Thus, Phil Watson of the Rangers was transferred to Montreal for the duration enabling him to play for the Habs while doing wartime duty in the area.

Other factors enabled the Canadiens to overcome their rivals as few teams have, before or since. They obtained a marvelous goalie, Bill

Durnan, who had been previously rejected by the Maple Leafs. Ambidextrous — he would hold his goalie stick in either hand, depending on the occasion — Durnan was a veritable marvel between the pipes and might easily have been the toast of Montreal were it not for a galvanic French-Canadian who previously had been thought to be too brittle for the majors.

Maurice Richard played right wing on a line with center Elmer Lach and left wing Toe Blake. The "Punch Line," as they were known, became the dominant trio of its time and helped the Habs to a top-heavy 38-5-7 record. Durnan won the Vezina Trophy and was immediately hailed as one of the best goalies since Brimsek was a rookie. "Bill had the size," said Canadiens manager Tommy Gorman, "but he also was as fast as they come, and a terrific team leader."

Like so many first place clubs, the Canadiens suffered a letdown in the playoffs, but only for a moment. They lost the first game of the opening round to Toronto but then got their act together and swept the next four straight and the series. The Habs then topped Chicago in four for a well-deserved Stanley Cup.

While Richard did not win a trophy that season, he did win the hearts of Montrealers, particularly in Game Two of the Toronto series. The man they would soon call the "Rocket" scored all five goals in the 5-1 Canadiens win.

The major tragedy of the era was the passing of Frank Calder who had been NHL president since its inception in 1917. Calder, who was sixty-six when he died in February 1943, was succeeded by Red Dutton, onetime manager of the Americans.

Dutton remained chief executive through the 1944-45 season which unquestionably marked a low water mark in terms of artistry. Youthful talent was scrounged up wherever possible. In the case of the Toronto Maple Leafs, the goaltending situation was so grave that a youngster afflicted with ulcers — surely the worst ailment for the nervous job of puck stopping — was hired to play for Toronto. Frank McCool nevertheless played all 50 games for the Maple Leafs, his ailment notwithstanding and posted a commendable 3.22 goals against average, which helped him earn the Calder Trophy as rookie of the year.

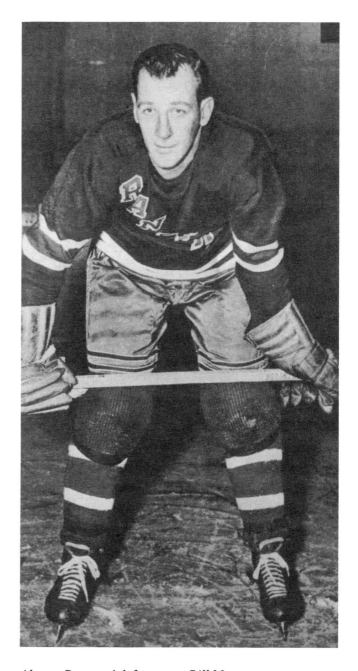

Above: Rangers' defenseman Bill Moe was a master of the hip check.

In terms of competence no goalie out-played Montreal's Bill Durnan who won the Vezina Trophy with a 2.42 goals against average. That was one of several reasons why Les Canadiens overwhelmed the regular season with a 38-8-4 mark. Another was the emergence of Maurice Richard as the league's most electrifying forward since Howie Morenz.

The Rocket was unusual in that he played right wing although he was a left handed shot. As a result, Richard developed a backhand drive that was harder to stop than most traditional forehand shots. Of course, The Rocket could shoot from virtually any angle and finished the season in the most spectacular manner possible, with 50 goals in 50 games. Richard finished

Above: Leafs' captain Syl Apps scores a playoff goal against "Sugar" Jim Henry of the Rangers.

Opposite page: Apps, a hero in Toronto throughout the Leaf-dominant forties, was elected to the Hall of Fame in 1961.

second in scoring behind teammate Elmer Lach. Toe Blake, third man on the Punch Line, wound up in third place on the list.

Because of the Canadiens overall balance they entered the 1945 playoffs as one of the heaviest of favorites. But McCool out dueled Durnan 1-0 in the playoff opener, setting the Habs back on their heels. They never fully recovered and bowed out of the series in six games.

McCool then shut out the Red Wings by successive scores of 1-0, 2-0 and 1-0 for what appeared to be an easy Toronto sweep. But just as quickly, the Detroiters swept the next three games setting the stage for a gripping final match. With the game tied 1-1 late in the third period, Babe Pratt of the Leafs scored a power play goal to ensure a 2-1 win and another Stanley Cup for Toronto.

Not long after the playoffs were completed Germany surrendered unconditionally to Allied forces and by the time the 1945-46 season was to begin, the Japanese had surrendered as well. The conclusion of World War II guaranteed a flood of returning players from all ends of the globe and the likelihood that NHL quality would soon achieve pre-war levels.

However, this was not necessarily the case, as the Rangers soon learned. Players who had starred on their 1940 championship club either were unavailable or unable to acclimatize themselves to big-league play. Defenseman and captain Art Coulter, who had served in the U.S. Coast Guard (and played for the Cutters) simply did not return to the NHL. Defenseman Muzz Patrick attempted a comeback and failed. The once-vaunted forward line of Neil and Mac Colville with Alex Shibicky was a shambles. Mac and Alex had lost their zip while Neil moved back to a defensive position where he finished his career.

Other clubs endured similar adjustment

roblems. Frankie Brimsek returned from his
.S. Coast Guard stint but his pre-war reflexes
ere not the same although he did manage a
.26 goals against average over 34 games in
945-46 with the second place Bruins.

Still another tragedy of war was the New
ork Americans. Manager Red Dutton, who
ould be succeeded as NHL President by
larence Sutherland Campbell, had been prom-
ed an opportunity to revive his Amerks and
ave them play in a proposed new arena in
rooklyn. Dutton thought he had league back-
g — not to mention the previous promise —
ut was rebuffed by the Rangers who wanted a
onopoly on New York hockey.

Dutton: "I told the NHL, 'I've talked to
eople in Brooklyn. They've got a site and
hey're ready to put up a $7 million building as
oon as I get the word from here...' I look around
he room and nobody's looking at me, and I get
he message. 'Gentlemen,' I said to the gover-
ors, 'You can stick your franchise up your ass.'
gathered up my papers and left."

The Americans passed into history and the
HL entered the post-war era with six teams
nd the prospects for full houses around the
ircuit. Factories still were busy, fans had money
n their pockets and the prospects of better
ockey lured them into the buildings.

Certainly, the hockey was a cut above the
vartime average even though many stars had
et to be mustered out of the armed forces. One
f the most attractive of the new faces belonged
o Edgar Laprade who had consistently refused
rofessional contracts up until now because of
is predilection for playing amateur hockey at
is home in Port Arthur, Ontario. Frank Boucher
inally persuaded Laprade to sign with the Rang-
rs and the center labelled "A Bearcat On The
rowl" proceeded to win the Calder Trophy.

The slightly-built Laprade was one of sev-
ral lightweights who demonstrated that

hockey was as much a game of skill and speed
as it was of brawn and physical play. Ditto for
Max Bentley, the Chicago center who led the
league in scoring and won the Hart Trophy for
a surprising potent Blackhawks squad. The
"Pony Line" of Max, brother Doug and Bill
"Wee Willie" Mosienko drove the enemy to
distraction with their adroit puck maneuvering.

Chicago took on the league-leading (28-
17-5) Canadiens in the opening round and despite the Pony League were no match for the
Punch Liners and Vezina Trophy-winner
(again) Bill Durnan. The Blackhawks were disposed of in four straight one-sided games
whereupon the Habs needed only five games
to oust the Bruins, four-games-to-one.

Normalcy returned to big-time hockey in
1946-47. By this time all the servicemen had
been assimilated into the NHL lineups, had

retired or finished their careers in the minors. Widespread farm systems were re-established and an infusion of crisp rookies gave the NHL a tang it hadn't savored since the start of the decade.

Toronto hailed a crew-cut right wing, Howie Meeker, whose life nearly was ended by an exploding grenade during his wartime tour of duty. Maple Leafs coach Hap Day placed Meeker on a line with gifted center Ted "Teeder" Kennedy and left wing Vic Lynn. They were anointed the "Kid Line" with apologies to the original trio of Busher Jackson, Charlie Conacher and Joe Primeau.

The returned war hero Conn Smythe was determined to rebuild his Leafs so that they could dethrone the vaunted Canadiens. Smythe's formula was a blend of rookies that included defensemen Bashin' Bill Barilko, Garth Boesch, Jim Thomson and Gus Mortson. The rookies would mature under the guidance of veterans like captain and center Syl Apps, Nick Metz, Harry Watson and goalie Turk Broda.

Nobody expected Smythe's skaters to accomplish very much in 1946-47 but they had a rare exuberance and a fair amount of talent; enough to guarantee a second place finish behind another expert Canadiens team (34-16-10) that showed no sign of wilting.

The Toronto-Montreal rivalry was embellished when Smythe's able lieutenant Frank Selke, Sr. left the Leafs fold for Montreal where he took on the job of managing director of the Canadiens. Smythe never masked the fact that he resented Selke's departure.

An inevitable clash between the Leafs and Canadiens developed when each club won its opening playoff round, against the Red Wings and Bruins, respectively. The finals seemed academic, based on the Game One result — 6-0 for the Habs. However, the one-sided score gave the victors a false sense of security.

Day's Leafs were extraordinarily resilient and rebounded for a 4-0 victory that was marred by Rocket Richard's stick attacks against Bill Ezinicki and Vic Lynn. The Rocket was fined $250 and suspended for the next game in which Toronto won, 4-2. Syl Apps scored a sudden death winner to stake the Leafs to a three game to one lead but Montreal rallied for a 3-1 edge in Game Five. The sixth and final game at Maple Leaf Gardens was settled when Ted Kennedy broke a 1-1 tie in the third period with a long, low shot. From that point on Turk Broda's goaltending was invincible and the Leafs skated off with the Cup, a most improbable event for a very underrated team.

Smythe more than anyone realized that the victory was an aberration of sorts and that Montreal monopolized the overall talent. "I knew that what we needed to get over the hump was a top center to go along with Kennedy and Apps," said the Major.

The object of Smythe's affection was Max Bentley who still teamed with brother Doug and Bill Mosienko on a Blackhawks team that couldn't get out of the cellar. To obtain Bentley the Toronto boss put together an enormous talent package consisting of an entire forward line, The Flying Forts (Gaye Stewart, Gus Bodnar and Bud Poile), as well as two promising defensemen, Ernie Dickens and Bob Goldham. It was an offer Chicago manager Bill Tobin could not refuse and the deal was consummated in November 1947.

Max Bentley admitted that he was crushed over the split with brother Doug and had trouble adjusting to his Toronto surroundings but once he did, the Maple Leafs not only found their groove but surpassed the Canadiens and finished first with a 32-15-13 record. "This," said Smythe who was not given to overstatement, "was the best Toronto club I ever had."

The observation was underlined during

playoffs. First, the Leafs defeated the Bruins in a bristling five game series and then erased the hated Red Wings in four straight. So strong was the Leafs offense that the productive Bentley was relegated to third line duty behind Apps and Kennedy.

Conversely, the Blackhawks got nowhere despite the infusion of new talent from Toronto but the Rangers, at long last, finished fourth which was a milestone of sorts. This was the Blueshirts' first playoff berth since 1942 before enlistments broke up a first-place team.

The Maple Leafs were considered a club that could finish first for at least two more seasons but that appraisal was drastically altered when the revered captain Syl Apps prematurely retired though in his prime. Apps' absence would create a major gap in the Toronto attack and make room for a change in the balance of power. The Red Wings with a new Production Line of Ted Lindsay, Sid Abel and Gordie Howe rose to the top of the heap fol-

Below: The Leafs didn't win every game — here Boston's Paul Ronty (20) and Johnny Peirson (23) score a 1948 goal against Broda, while Joe Klukay and Gus Mortson move in.

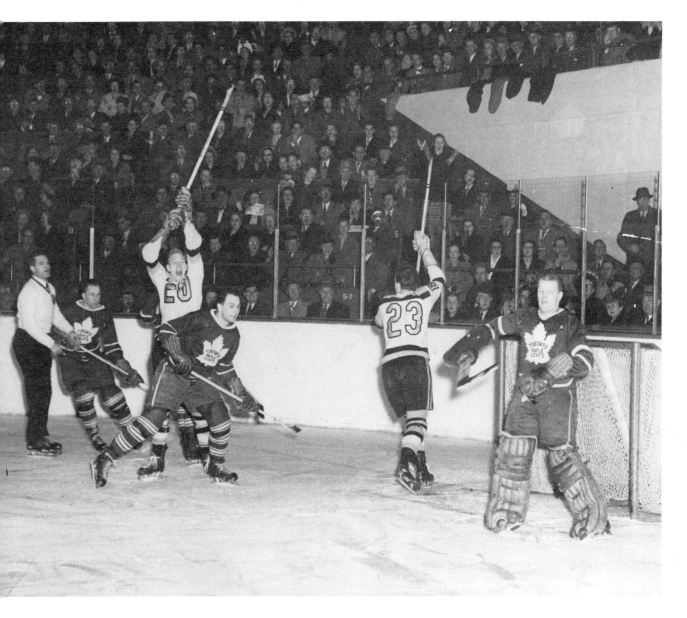

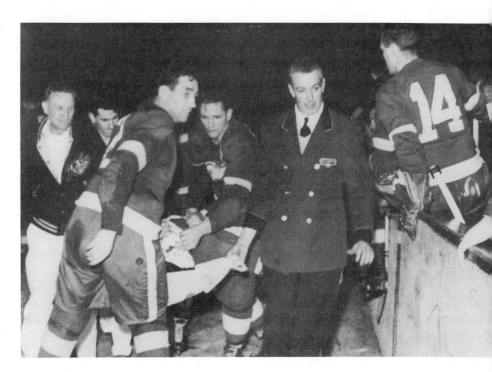

Right: Gordie Howe's closest brush with death occurred in the opening playoff game between his Red Wings and the Maple Leafs, at the close of the 1949-50 season. Detroit players charged that Leaf captain "Teeder" Kennedy deliberately butt-ended Howe, but league president Clarence Campbell exonerated the Toronto player.

lowed by Boston and Montreal. The Rangers and Chicago, who had become regular doormats, were out of the running again.

Were it not for the mediocre play of New York and the Blackhawks, the Leafs might well have missed the playoffs with their 22-25-13 record. But they squeezed in, eight points behind third place Montreal and then scripted an astonishing revival.

First, they disposed of Boston in a bitter five-game set, qualifying them to meet a Detroit club which had sweated through a tough seven-gamer with Montreal. When crack defenseman Gus Mortson was sidelined in Game One of the finals with a broken leg, the Leafs chances dropped even lower than they had been at the outset but now Toronto was playing in the form that had won two straight

Cups. They topped Detroit 5-3 in Game One and then reeled off scores of 4-2, 2-0 and 7-2. Never before had an NHL team won three straight Stanley Cups.

Despite the establishment of Toronto as the league's first hockey dynasty — dynasty is defined as winning three or more Stanley Cups in succession — both Detroit and Montreal were right up there on a competitive level. The Red Wings and Canadiens had created formidable farm systems and were rapidly developing new stars, the latest of which was Gordie Howe in the Motor City.

The beginning of another decade would be highlighted by intense warfare among the Big Three with headline-making episodes some of which would border on the tragic, among them the near-death of Howe.

CHAPTER SIX

An Era of Greatness

IF THERE WERE TWO singular elements of the 1950s they would be the collision of stars, both individual and collective.

On the individual level fans were constantly arguing the merits of "Who's better — Maurice Richard or Gordie Howe."

On the collective side, warfare raged throughout the decade between their respective teams, the Canadiens and Red Wings.

The 1950s began with Detroit on top and ended with Montreal ruling the league as no team ever has before or since. Eruptions between the clubs both in regular season games and the post-season playoffs were epic in their proportions, primarily because of the Howe-Richard confrontations but also because of innumerable other nuances that created such high drama.

No less relevant was the surfacing of the Rangers as a considerable Stanley Cup threat in 1950 followed by a long, depressing, non-playoff period matched only by the Blackhawks who appeared once, in 1953, and then rapidly faded from view. One of Chicago's few claims

to fame occurred on March 23, 1952 when Bill Mosienko scored three goals in 21 seconds — a league record likely never to be broken — against, who else, the Rangers.

Perhaps most important of all was the element of overall league crisis for the NHL actually was in danger of collapse or a severe curtailment of its six-team roster.

Following World War II, prosperity reigned throughout the continent and teams played to capacity or, at worst, near-full houses. But the advent of the 1950s brought with it the new entertainment medium, television, and with tv came considerable competition for the hockey fan's dollar. Attendance began to significantly slip in Boston, Chicago and New York. For a time it appeared that both the Bruins and Blackhawks might actually fold and, eventually, the league itself intervened with a "Help The Poor" campaign that resurrected all the weak clubs.

The decade opened with the Rangers uncharacteristically squeaking into fourth place and then driving through the opening 1950

Above: Maurice "Rocket" Richard was one of the most intense competitors in hockey history. One of his arch rivals was Ivan "The Terrible" Irwin of the Rangers. Their respective eyes say it all about the fury of hockey in the 50's.

playoff round with a five-game (4-1) triumph over the Canadiens. It marked the final series for venerable goalie Bill Durnan who turned the pads over to young Gerry McNeil for the final two games.

Meanwhile, the Red Wings and defending champion Maple Leafs were engaged in what arguably was the most bitter series ever played. In Game One at Detroit's Olympia Stadium, Red Wings' right wing Gordie Howe — then the most promising forward in the league — collided with Toronto captain Ted Kennedy at center ice and plummeted head first to the ice and the boards.

The Leafs argued that Kennedy merely was sidestepping Howe's intended bodycheck and hardly made contact whereas the Wings charged that Kennedy deliberately butt-ended

Howe, dispatching him harshly to the ice. Whatever the case — no video replay was availabl‍ for perusal and no definitive answers ever wer‍ provided — Howe was seriously injured. H‍ suffered a fractured nose, cheekbone and a brain concussion of such severity that an emergency operation was performed to relieve pressur‍ from a broken blood vessel in his head.

For a short time it appeared that How‍ might not survive and family members wer‍ rushed to his bedside. In the meantime, the Re‍

Despite this apparent disadvantage, the Rangers extended their foe to a seventh and final game which then went into double overtime before a little-known bench-warmer from Braeburn, Pennsylvania, named Pete Babando beat New York goalie Charlie Rayner for the Cup-winning score.

While Howe recovered from his near-fatal injury to star again in 1950-51, another tragedy would blemish what should have been a joyful year which concluded with a rousing playoff finale between Montreal and Toronto. The five-game set was tagged the "Sudden Death Series" because every one of the contests went into overtime.

Toronto led the series three to one as the teams took the ice on April 21, 1951 at Maple Leaf Gardens. Montreal nursed a 2-1 lead into the final minute of the third period when the Leafs rallied for a goal by Tod Sloan with 32 seconds left. In overtime Toronto defenseman

Wings, convinced that Kennedy deliberately harmed their young ace, sought revenge in Game Two. The match was pockmarked with free-for-alls which set the tone for the remainder of the series which went the full seven games until Leo Reise, Jr., scored the winner in overtime.

That pitted the Rangers against the Red Wings in a curious final round. Ousted from their Madison Square Garden home by the Ringling Brothers' Circus, the Blueshirts chose Maple Leaf Gardens in Toronto as the site of two "home" games.

Above: Ranger fans had little to cheer about in the early 1950s, but one thing in their favour was the scoring of "Little Wally" Hergesheimer, a right winger from Winnipeg.

Right: In his prime in the early and middle fifties, "Leapin' Lou" Fontinato was one of the most feared defensemen in the NHl. Fontinato outfought most of the NHL's tough guys — until he challenged Gordie Howe.

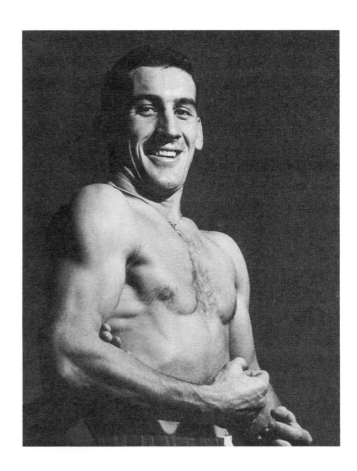

Left: This bout at Madison Square Garden during the 1958 season effectively ended Fontinato's career as a tough guy. Howe, shown here in a white jersey behind the net, broke Fontinato's nose and otherwise humbled him. Fontinato is hunched over — on the receiving end of a flurry of Howe uppercuts — in front of referee Art Skov.

Bill Barilko — little known for his scoring prowess — whacked a long shot over goalie Gerry McNeil at 2:53 of sudden death to settle matters.

Barilko, already a popular figure, became a national hero in Canada and was earmarked for a long and successful career. But later that summer he embarked on camping trip in the Northern Ontario woods with a dentist friend who piloted a small plane. The aircraft disappeared over the dense bush country and despite heroic attempts to locate the plane, the search was eventually cancelled and Barilko given up for lost. Years later the wreckage was found with both bodies still in the craft.

Not only did the Leafs lose a promising defenseman but also the spark of their dressing room. Without him, they were a different team and began a long slide that would not be reversed until the arrival of George "Punch" Imlach as ruler of the team.

With Toronto out of the way, the battle fo league domination raged between Detroit an Montreal. Through the 1950s, including th 1958-59 season, the Red Wings finished first n less than seven times, yet they were only abl to win four Stanley Cups. The Canadiens fin ished first only three times but won the Cuɩ five times in the same period.

Naturally, both teams were oozing witl talent. The Red Wings top unit, the "Productior Line," featured Sid Abel at center with Howɩ and Ted Lindsay. Upon the retirement of Abel Alex Delvecchio proved a super replacemen and, later, Norm Ullman succeeded Delvecchio The Red Wings defense was anchored by Rec Kelly, one of the few rushing backliners, anc Marcel Pronovost while the goaltending, in the early Fifties, featured a youthful Terry Sawchuk

The Canadiens, relying on an abundan farm system, introduced a spate of new face: including goalie Jacques Plante, defensemer oug Harvey and Tom Johnson and such out-anding forwards as Jean Beliveau, Dickie Moore, Bernie Geoffrion and Henri "Pocket ocket" Richard, kid brother of the Rocket.

Not only were the Habs artistic but they ere innovative as well. The boisterous eoffrion introduced the slapshot as an effec-ve offensive weapon whereas the wrist shot nd backhander had been traditionally used. Iante became the first goalie to regularly roam om his crease to field pucks behind the net for is defensemen and later chose to wear a face nask as a protective piece although goaltenders ad shunned such a device for years.

But the Montrealers still were in a state of eorganization in the early 1950s while the Red

Wings boasted a set roster. When Detroit won the Stanley Cup sweeping all eight games in 1952 it was freely predicted that Howe & Co. had the goods to run off at least three more championships.

And so it seemed to be the case when the 1953 playoffs opened and the Wings trashed Boston 7-0 in the first game. But the Bruins rebounded for a 5-3 victory in Game Two and then proceeded to stifle the Howe line and won the series in six games for one of the biggest upsets in playoff history. Boston gave Montreal a brief scare in the finals before succumbing in five games.

The traditionally woeful Blackhawks enjoyed one brief moment of joy during the 1952-

Left: The Detroit Red Wings' dynasty of the early fifties was the work of General Manager Jack "Jolly Jawn" Adams, who had once been a star player in his own right. Adams launched the careers of such Hall-of-Famers as Gordie Howe, Ted Lindsay, and Red Kelly.

53 season when they challenged Les Canadiens in the opening playoff round. That was the year in which Sid Abel moved over from Detroit to become Chicago's playing coach. The aging center not only did wonders on the bench but also added considerable zest to the attack. The Blackhawks got another boost from goalie Al Rollins who previously had starred for Toronto.

In a series that literally mesmerized Montreal fans, the Blackhawks rebounded from two straight defeats to win three games in a row and stand but one victory away from eliminating the vaunted Habs. Desperate for a change, Montreal coach Dick Irvin replaced veteran Gerry McNeil with rookie goalie Jacques Plante who blanked Chicago 3-0 in Game Six and then held the Hawks to one goal in Game Seven while the Montrealers scored four. The Habs then dispatched Boston in five games.

Although attendance sagged in spots, the hockey quality remained high in the six team

league. The intensity of competition frequentl led to brawling. Particular attention was pai to Rocket Richard whose temper outbursts wer as legendary as his scoring feats.

A number of Richardian outbursts brough complaints from rival managers who asserte that NHL President Clarence Campbell wa too lenient with the Rocket. The Canadien countered that their star was being unfairl abused and not sufficiently protected by th rulebook nor the referees. Eventually, thi would result in one of hockey's more memora ble explosions.

But before the Richardian Riot, anothe episode brought Campbell to the fore. On De

Above: Maurice Richard found a new center in 1955 when his kid brother Henri (left) joined the Canadiens. The "Rocket" and the "Pocket Rocket" proved a formidable pair.

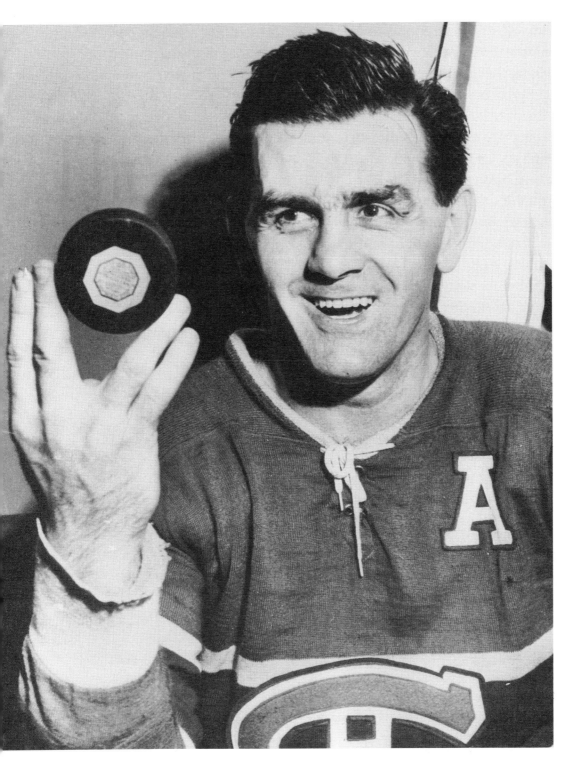

Left: On December 19, 1954, Maurice Richard became the first player to score 400 career goals. The historic tally was registered at Chicago Stadium in a 4-2 win over the Blackhawks.

ember 20, 1953 the Canadiens visited Madison Square Garden where they were beaten 3-1. Late in the second period a scuffle began along the boards involving several players on both teams. Out of it came Geoffrion and Rangers rookie Ron Murphy. When the pair moved to center ice, Bernie Geoffrion swung his stick baseball-fashion and clobbered Murphy in the head, sending him to the ice, a bloody mess. The Ranger suffered a broken jaw and concussion. Campbell suspended Geoffrion from playing in the remaining seven games scheduled between the two teams while Murphy was suspended from the next four games between them.

Try as they might, the Rangers couldn't lift themselves into a playoff berth. In 1953-54 they tried yet another extraordinary ploy. First, they signed Hall of Famer Max Bentley, who had retired from the NHL after the 1952-53 season with the Maple Leafs, and lured him back as a part-time power play specialist. Then, on January 21, 1954, Rangers manager Frank Boucher lured Max's older brother, Doug, out of retirement and teamed him with Max and another aging ace, Edgar Laprade, who also had been coaxed into returning to the NHL. On that night they were sensational, beating Boston, 8-3, as the Rangers made a stirring move for a playoff spot. But the Bentleys faded at the end and, once more, New York was out of contention.

In the spring of 1954 Detroit and Montreal faced off in the first of three consecutive Stanley Cup finals. The series went down to the wire with the seventh game tied at one and moving into overtime. With almost four-and-a-half minutes gone, Detroit's Tony Leswick fired an innocent shot at Gerry McNeil. The goalie was about to make the save when his defenseman Doug Harvey reached up in an attempt to deflect it harmlessly into the corner. But Harvey only got a piece of the rubber and it bounced over the defenseman's glove and into the net for the Cup-winner.

A year later the same clubs fought tooth and nail down to the wire. This time the Habs appeared to have an edge until mid-March when the Canadiens visited Boston Garden. Tempers were raw, especially between Maurice Richard and Boston defenseman Hal Laycoe. They finally battled and when linesman Cliff Thompson (himself a former Bruin) intervened, Richard flattened the official.

After studying the incident — and considering Richard's past NHL misdemeanors —

Campbell suspended Richard for the remainder of the season *and* the entire Stanley Cup playoffs. It was an unprecedented move and a colossal blow to both the Canadiens club and Richard himself who was positioned to win his first ever scoring championship.

The decision was handed down on March 17, 1955 when the Red Wings were scheduled

Above: A former star with the Toronto Maple Leafs, "Gentleman Joe" Primeau became one of hockey's most successful bench leaders. He is the only man ever to have coached a Memorial (Junior) Cup champion, an Allan (Senior) Cup champion, and a Stanley Cup winner. The latter he accomplished in 1951 with the Leafs.

to play the Habs in Montreal. Long before game time angry crowds began demonstrating in front of The Forum and by the time the opening puck was dropped it was clear that trouble was brewing. The explosion was detonated when Campbell, himself, arrived at his seat. He was almost immediately assaulted by fans whereupon a tear gas cannister was set off, sending thousands of spectators scurrying for exits. The game was cancelled and forfeited to the Red Wings while Campbell was hurriedly escorted to safety.

Meanwhile, a full-scale riot erupted along Montreal's main drag, St. Catherine Street West. Bands of hoodlums smashed windows, set fire to newstands and generally behaved like louts. Richard, eventually, appeared on radio and television urging calm among his followers.

Thoroughly demoralized, the Canadiens lost first place to the Red Wings while Richard's teammate, Bernie Geoffrion scored enough points — though some of his peers thought he

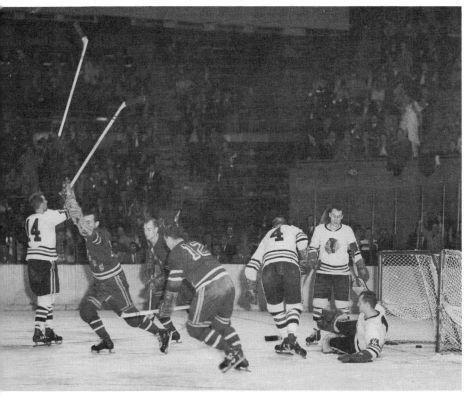

Above: It is unlikely that any player will match Bill Mosienko's feat of scoring three goals in 21 seconds. The Blackhawks' captain did it on the final night (March 23) of the 1951-52 season against Rangers' goalie Lorne Anderson.

Left: The sticks are flying in anger and glee. Glen Skov (14) of the Blackhawks raises his in frustration while Parker MacDonald (stick in the air) hails a late Ranger goal. The others are (left to right) Dave Creighton, Andy Hebenton (12, Elmer Vasko (4) Pierre Pilote and goalie Al Rollins.

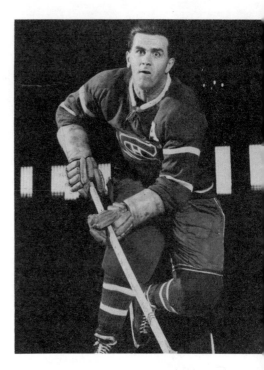

On St. Patrick's Day (March 17, 1955), a riot broke out at Montreal's Forum after a fan tossed a tear gas bomb at ice level. The episode occurred shortly after NHL President Clarence Campbell announced the suspension of Maurice "Rocket" Richard (shown above in uniform and at left wearing fedora in the seats) for the remaining games of the season and the playoffs, for belting linesman Cliff Thompson. The Rocket was leading the league in scoring at the time, but lost the title to teammate Bernie "Boom Boom" Geoffrion.

ould have passed them up for the Rocket's
ke — to take the scoring title away from
ichard.

Despite the hardship, Montreal made it to
e finals with the Red Wings. Once again, the
ries went the seven-game limit, concluding
Olympia Stadium. Without Richard's clutch
al-scoring, the Canadiens couldn't quite keep
p and went out 3-1 as Alex Delvecchio led
etroit with a pair of goals.

The Richard Riot had both short and
ngterm ramifications. Canadiens manager
ank Selke, Sr. believed that the Rocket's tan-
ums were at least in part encouraged by coach
ick Irvin. With Selke's blessing, Irvin left Mon-
eal and took a job leading the Blackhawks
though at the time the coach was in the early
ages of a cancer that would eventually take
s life.

Irvin was replaced by Toe Blake, Richard's
rmer linemate who always had a calming

influence on the Rocket. The change was extraordinarily beneficial to Richard and the
Canadiens as a group. They took an early lead
in the race and finished with 45 wins and only
15 losses with ten ties for exactly 100 points, a
good 24 ahead of Detroit.

Montreal's scoring power was awesome.
Jean Beliveau won the scoring title as well as
the Hart Trophy while Jacques Plante grabbed
the Vezina Trophy. The Canadiens third liners
often were better than first-liners on other clubs
and the Habs power play — Beliveau, Geoffrion,
Harvey, and the Richards — was awesome. In
addition to the scorers, Montreal had the best
cornerman in the league, Bert Olmstead, and,
of course, Plante's impeccable goaltending
which improved with the season.

As the Canadiens climbed, the Red Wings
sagged a bit. The turnabout came when manager Jack Adams decided to trade goalie Terry
Sawchuk to Boston and replace him with rookie

Left: In his prime, during the early 1950s, Terry Sawchuk was one of the greatest goalies in hockey history. In this arresting photo, Ed Kullman of the Rangers flies over Detroit defenseman Leo Reise Jr. after getting a shot away at Sawchuk.

Glenn Hall. True, Hall won the Calder Trophy but the Red Wings were not the same team without Sawchuk and would never win a Stanley Cup with Hall — or anyone else for that matter — in goal.

Montreal disposed of Detroit in five games of the final for what was to be an unprecedented Stanley Cup run. The Red Wings mounted one last threat, finishing first in the 1956-57 season, six points ahead of Montreal. But any designs Jack Adams had on another Stanley Cup were smashed when a shot by Boston's Vic Stasiuk hit Glenn Hall in the face. While the goalie was able to return to action, he was not the same — at least not in Adams' eyes — as Boston upset Detroit in a manner reminiscent of the 1953 series. With Detroit out of the way, Montreal breezed to a five-game final series triumph and a second straight Stanley Cup.

Attendance began to show healthy signs of recovery in the late 1950s as did the fortunes of the once hapless Rangers but the same couldn't be said for the Blackhawks who finished last for the fourth straight year in 1956-57.

With that in mind, as well as unexpected turmoil generated by players, the league underwent another metamorphosis. It began with a mini-player revolt launched by some of the NHL's most prominent individuals. Led by Ted Lindsay, the stickhandlers believed that they were being underpaid by ownership and chose to organize a union.

Owners were suitably furious and responded in the finest strikebreaking tradition by punishing the culprits. Lindsay, who had been a Red Wings stalwart all his life, was dealt to the lowly Hawks as was another organizer Jim Thomson of the Maple Leafs. Dismayed with Hall's playoff effort, Adams shipped the goalie to Chicago as well while Sawchuk returned to the Motor City.

While the bust-the-union movement wasn't entirely successful, it did succeed in frightening many potential union members and, in time, the owners emerged the victors. If nothing else, the revolt sufficiently bolstered the Blackhawks to move them out of the cellar on the strength of Hall's exceptional goaltending. The once

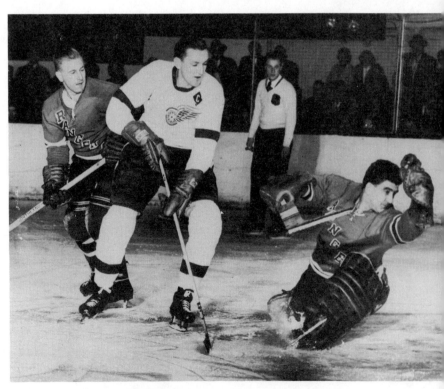

Right: Sid Abel (center) was nicknamed "Ole Bootnose" by his Red Wings teammates. Abel centered the famed "Production Line" with Gordie Howe and Ted Lindsay. Here he gets past Ranger forward Eddie Kullman and fires a backhander past goalie Chuck Rayner.

Left: The Montreal Canadiens won an unprecedented five straight Stanley Cups from 1956 through to 1960. Three of their stars are shown here defusing an attack by Detroit's Nick Mickoski. They include Doug Harvey (left, moving the puck out of danger), goalie Jacques Plante (center) and forward Don Marshall (right). Partially obscured behind Plante is defenseman Jean-Guy Talbot.

roud Maple Leafs, torn with inner turmoil, nished last in a season marked with unusual vents.

One of the more positive moves was the ruins' decision to promote left wing Willie 'Ree to the big club. The first Black player ver skate in the NHL only played a pair of ames for the Beantowners — he returned again 1960-61 for 43 games — but he did impress with his speed and stickhandling ability. Another milestone was achieved when veteran broadcaster Foster Hewitt turned his play-by-play duties over to his son, Bill, who had been apprenticing for several years. And still another milestone was the 500th goal scored by Rocket Richard.

Montreal romped to another first place finish, 19 points ahead of a surprisingly strong New York sextet. Orchestrated by fiery coach Phil Watson, the Rangers at last had a truly threatening club. Gump Worsley provided more than adequate goaltending while such defensemen as Bill Gadsby, Lou Fontinato and Jack Evans comprised a granite defense. While

Left: Fleming Mackell (left) was one of the NHL's fastest players in the 1950s. Here he tests Chicago goalie Al Rollins at Boston Garden. Blackhawk Pierre Pilote slides in to help while Boston's Larry Regan looms in the background.

the New Yorkers couldn't match the Canadiens overall firepower, they did have sharpshooters such as Camille "The Eel" Henry, Andy Bathgate, Dean Prentice and Dave Creighton.

"There was a time," said Henry, "when we thought we were good enough to go all the way."

Unfortunately for the Rangers, Boston got in the way. In what was a vicious semi-final, the Bruins ousted New York in six games while the Canadiens shellacked Detroit in four. Th[e] scrappy Bruins gave Montreal fits in the fina[l] before bowing out four games to two and Mo[n]treal became only the second team in NH[L] annals to have won three consecutive Stanle[y] Cups. (Toronto turned the trick in 1947, 194[8] and 1949).

The essence of the Canadiens' dominan[ce] was Rocket Richard's new discipline and ded[i]cation under coach Toe Blake. Richard explaine[d]

Right: The tight confines of Boston Garden produced crunching checks and short tempers. The home team defenseman Doug "Diesel" Mohns trades blows with Ralph Backstrom (6) of the Canadiens.

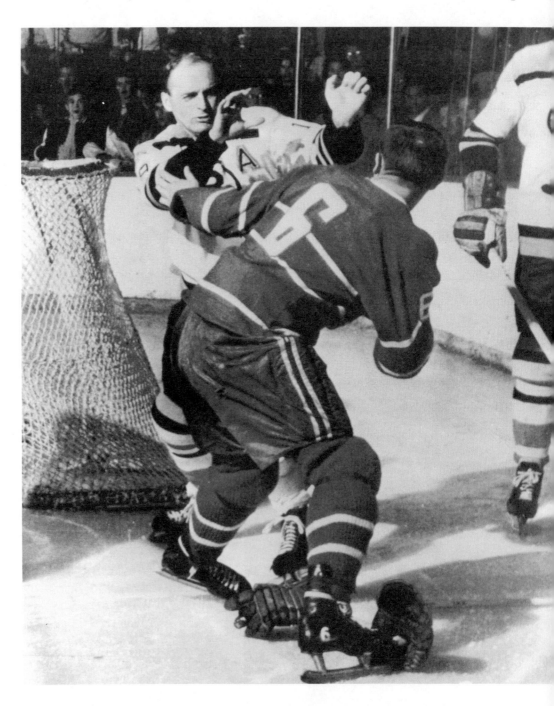

Above: By 1957 Gordie Howe had established himself as the NHL's most dominant forward. He is shown here breaking through the Boston defense to beat goalie Don Simmons during the 1957 playoffs. Teammate Norm Ullman is behind Howe. The other Bruins are defenseman Leo Boivin (20) and Fern Flaman in the rear.

Right: Howe flips his patented forehand past goalie Glenn Hall of the Blackhawks in 1958 action.

in his own words what make the Habs tick:

"Each year my kid brother kept getting better and better which partly explains why we were able to take one Stanley Cup after another. Conn Smythe of the Leafs once said the key to a team's success is `strength down the center' and we sure had it. There was Henri, Beliveau, and young Ralph Backstrom but Henri and Beliveau were one-two, depending on how you like your centers. It's hard to compare the two because their styles differed so much. My brother was a better puck-carrier and a better skater and he took more of the rough stuff than Beliveau, even though he was much smaller. Beliveau, of course, had been a better scorer, but I always felt that Henri was sort of skating

in Beliveau's shadow and he really shouldn' have been. Henri was on the puck all the tim and if he didn't have the puck, you knew h was always around. His one mistake alway was not shooting enough.

"I liked Jacques Plante better as a playe than as a personality. He popped off to th press and never seemed to want to take th blame for anything, especially when he wa beaten and looked bad. As a result some of th

Below: During the 1950s the Rangers were so bad that they were willing to try anything for a win — even hypnotism. Doctor David Tracy works over (left to right) Tony Leswick, Ed Slowinski, Chuck Rayner, and Edgar Laprade. The Rangers managed only a tie and Doctor Tracy was given his leave.

ayers developed a dislike for him. Eventually, the Canadiens traded him. If he'd been smart, he would have been a lot more careful with what he said, especially to his own teammates. He would have been better liked and would have lasted in Montreal a lot longer than he did. The record shows that he didn't get along with Dick Irvin and he didn't get along with Toe Blake; in New York, he didn't get along with Red Sullivan."

Plante was an independent free-thinker who fervently believed that the time had come for goaltenders to wear protective facial gear. Unfortunately, his coach, Toe Blake, believed in the macho theory and forbade its use until a

game at Madison Square Garden on November 1, 1959 when Plante was struck in the face by a puck fired by Andy Bathgate.

After being taken to the dressing room for extensive repairs, Plante vowed that he would not return unless Blake permitted him to don a plastic-type mask which he had been wearing in scrimmages and had been carrying with him to road games. Having no spare goalie — and, therefore, no choice — Blake reluctantly agreed.

Plante won the game and therefore the right to wear the mask in the ensuing contest. Again, he won and again and again and again until Blake finally conceded the issue and the mask became a permanent part of Plante's goaltending equipment.

At first, he seemed freakish among other mask-less goalies but, slowly, relentlessly, other netminders began experimenting with the protective device and, soon, the mask became *de rigeuer* among the puckstopping clan.

As good as he was without the mask, Plante

Below: Lorne "Gump" Worsley was one of the more colourful goalies of the 1950s. The New Yorker stops a Blackhawk thrust spearheaded by (left to right) Johnny Wilson, Wally Hergesheimer (7) and Ken Mosdell. The Rangers defenseman is Bill Gadsby with referee Gaye Stewart in the background.

Above: Jean Beliveau dekes Boston goalies Don Simmons to score for the Canadiens at Boston Garden in March 1957. It marked Beliveau's 30th goal of the campaign.

appeared even better with the security of a thick layer of plastic in front of his cheekbones, brow and chin. In 1958-59, Jacques totalled a league-leading nine shutouts and a 2.15 goals against average. On the other side of the ledger, the Canadiens' Dickie Moore led the league in scoring followed by Jean Beliveau.

At season's start, the Rangers loomed as the most threatening club to the Canadiens dominance but New York's general manager Muzz Patrick blundered on a number of trades that robbed his club of substance and character. He mistakenly dealt redoubtable defenseman Jack "Tex" Evans to Chicago, center Dave Creighton to Montreal and utility forward Guy Gendron to Boston.

The Blackhawks renaissance continued as goalie Glenn Hall received much needed blue line support. In addition to Evans, Chicago now had Pierre Pilote and Elmer "Moose" Vasko on defense as well as Dollard St.Laurent, who had been obtained from Montreal. Suddenly, the Blackhawks boasted one of the better blueline corps in the league.

Chicago's long-neglected farm system also began bearing fruit; the most appetizing of which was a Czech-born center who grew up in St.Catherines, Ontario. Stanislaus Gvoth — renamed Stan Mikita — along with Bobby Hull would form the best one-two scoring punch in Chicago since the days of the Bentley Brothers

Between riotous moments when he was
·lling dialect stories to his players and more
·rious times when he was at the blackboard,
·ach Rudy Pilous proved a tonic to the Chi-
·go players and the Blackhawks climbed all
·e way to third place which, for them, was a
·onumental achievement.

The Rangers had been expected to finish
· high as second and, in fact, they were in that
·fty position late in the season when the club
·acked under Phil Watson's incessant whip-
·ing. The *coup de grace* was supplied one evening
·fter a particularly trying game at Madison
·quare Garden in which the Rangers blew a
·im lead and had to settle for a tie.

Watson ordered his players back on to the
·e after the match and forced them through a
·ruelling skate until the Blueshirts were falling
·ver with exhaustion. "We never recovered af-
·r that night," said Camille Henry. "That extra
·orkout killed us for the season."

With two weeks remaining, the Rangers
·ill had a commanding nine point lead over

the Maple Leafs but Toronto finished strong
and actually eked out a fourth-place finish on
the final night of the season, beating Detroit
while the Rangers were losing to Montreal.
New York wound up in fifth and Detroit last.

The Blackhawks proved a worthy foe for
Montreal in one of the two semi-final rounds,
losing four games to two but not without making it close. After the sixth and final match at

Ranger Antics!
*Above: Ranger coach Muzz
Patrick , who's father had
coached the team in the 1920s
and 1930s, gets needed
adjustments to his jacket from
GM Frank Boucher. A young
Johnny Bower looks on.*

*Right: Hilda Chester gained
her fame as a Brooklyn
Dodger cowbell-toting fan at
Ebbets Field. When the
hockey season began she
moved to Madison Square
Garden where she was a loyal
member of the Rangers Fan
Club. Hilda is flanked by
Rangers coach at the time,
Phil Watson (left) and Fan
Club president Jacques Schiff.*

Chicago Stadium, NHL President Clarence Campbell told Ottawa Journal hockey writer Bill Westwick that he thought referee Red Storey froze when he failed to call a penalty shot against Montreal defenseman Al Langlois for tripping Bobby Hull. Campbell claimed that it was an off-the-record remark not meant for publication but Westwick understood otherwise and ran the piece. When Storey read Campbell's account in the next day's papers, he promptly resigned, causing no end of waves throughout the high command.

On the other front, Punch Imlach's upstart Maple Leafs ousted the Bruins in seven games. A team that appeared destined to miss the playoffs a few weeks earlier now was in the finals against a Canadiens club determined to become the first NHL organization ever to win four consecutive Stanley Cups.

Critics freely predicted a blowout for the young and generally inexperienced Maple Leafs but they were wrong. Imlach had his troops battling for every inch of ice and never in the five game set was Toronto embarrassed. Indeed, after losing the first two games at The Forum, the Leafs rebounded to take the Habs 3-2 at Maple Leaf Gardens before losing 3-2 and 5-3, respectively, to close out the series.

Montreal had its fourth consecutive Stanley Cup and a roster still bubbling with talent. Really, only one element of doubt surrounded the Habs future. The lion of winter, Maurice Richard, captain of the team, now was 38 years old. "I had been getting slower," The Rocket admitted, "and I knew I couldn't hang in very much longer, but I wanted to try one more season before I quit."

And that he did. So strong was the rest of the Canadiens lineup that manager Frank Selke Sr. had room for only one addition, talented young defenseman Jean-Claude Tremblay. Jacques Plante was a fixture in goal; Tom Johnson and Doug Harvey on defense and the usual set of bombers — Beliveau, Geoffrion, Henri Richard, et. al. — up front.

The challenge belonged to coach Toe Blake. Could he keep his perennial winners from becoming jaded? Would a clubhouse dissident such as Plante upset the camaraderie that had been so well established? Would Rocket Richard's age and added poundage prove so much of a detriment that he would slow down his young and sprightly linemates?

These were vexing questions for Blake but certainly not insoluble for the man who already was being hailed as the coach of the decade.

CHAPTER SEVEN

The Golden Years and Expansion

THE TURBULENT END to the 1958-59 regular season as well as the playoff results caused a long-term fallout that would reverberate through the early part of the next decade.

In the Rangers' case the franchise would require years to shake off the trauma of blowing the nine-point lead and the playoff berth to Toronto. Ultimately, coach Phil Watson was fingered for blame and was fired early in the 1959-60 campaign.

Conversely, the Maple Leafs late-season resurgence under Punch Imlach provided the Toronto organization with a vitality which it had not enjoyed since the halcyon days of Conn Smythe, Syl Apps and Turk Broda. Fortified with such outstanding young talents as Carl Brewer, Frank "Big M" Mahovlich, Bob Pulford, Ron Stewart and Bob Baun, the Torontonians would become a major presence throughout the 1960s.

The mercurial Imlach would confound his critics at every turn. Like Smythe before him, Imlach enjoyed distilling youth and veterans. Where Smythe employed Turk Broda in goal

during the late 1940s, Imlach went with retread Johnny Bower who, ironically, had been shed by the Rangers after posting a handsome 2.60 goals against average during the 1953-54 season. Bower had then been buried in the minors with the Cleveland Barons before being rescued by Imlach when others had rated him over-the-hill.

Imlach also signed older defensemen like Allan Stanley who once had been so reviled by New York fans that he literally was booed out of Madison Square Garden and a Rangers uniform in 1954. Another marvelous Imlachian move was his decision to take Red Kelly, who had spent his entire career playing defense for the Red Wings, and convert him to a center in his waning years. Undaunted, Kelly accepted the assignment and became the key pivot between Mahovlich and Nevin, arguably the best all-round line of the early 1960s.

No less impressive was a line contrived by Rudy Pilous in Chicago. The Blackhawks farm system had delivered him an exquisite prospect in left wing Bobby Hull. Rough around the

Above: Bobby Hull, the legendary "Golden Jet".   "... one of the best advertisements hockey ever had."

dges when he moved to the Windy City in the ate 1950s, Hull improved his skating to a point vhere he was virtually unstoppable when developing a full head of steam. But the core of Hull's arsenal was a shot that was unmatched or its speed and uncertainty.

The Hull drive was an outgrowth of Bernie Geoffrion's original invention, the slapshot. Introduced the previous decade, the slapshot was adapted by Andy Bathgate of the Rangers and one or two other players in the final years of the 950s. Still, most shooters relied on the traditional forehand wristshot and backhander.

In the early 1960s, Hull and teammate Stan Mikita perfected a method of rendering a curve on the traditional straight stick blade. Bobby and Stan soon were able to produce remarkably hard shots that often dipped and rose, depending on where the stick made contact with the rubber.

Hull was placed on a line with Bill Hay, a redheaded center of considerable creativity, and Murray Balfour, a former Canadien product who had a feisty nature that complemented the laconic nature of his teammates.

Pilous formed another formation with Mikita at center between fleet Ken Wharram and Chico Maki. In time it was dubbed the "Scooter Line" and would be in its way as effective as the Hull trio. One difference was the charismatic nature of Hull. Adonis-like with his flowing blond hair — he wasn't nicknamed The Golden Jet for nothing — Hull savored the crowds and rarely if ever shunned an autograph request. "He was," said Pilous, "one of the best advertisements hockey ever had. And could he ever shoot the puck."

Hull led the league in scoring (39-42-81) over the 1959-60 season, finishing a point ahead of Boston's Bronco Horvath and seven ahead of

Left: Hockey's greatest dynasty, the Montreal Canadiens, shown here with the Cup in 1960, their fifth consecutive championship.

Montreal's majestic Jean Beliveau. Significantly, Rocket Richard played in only 51 games and amassed only 19 goals and 16 assists for 35 points putting deep down in the scoring list.

No matter. Montreal ran away with the pennant race. At mid-season Toe Blake had his Habs positioned in first place with a 22-6-7 mark, a fat 11 points ahead of runner-up Detroit. When the 70-game schedule was completed, the Habs had 92 points (40-18-12) which gave them a 13-point cushion over second place Toronto. (Detroit slipped to a fourth place 67

points.) Plante produced only three shutouts yet still managed the best goals against average (2.54 to runner-up Glenn Hall's 2.57) and remained at the very top of his goaltending game although his relations with management were becoming more frayed by the season.

When Montreal and Chicago collided in the first round, the Blackhawks no longer were taken lightly although the first two games were played at The Forum. The Hawks made a game of it both times but in each contest, lost by a 4-3 score. After that it was all a breeze for the Habs.

Right: The "Pocket Rocket." If the yardstick of success in the NHL is winning the Stanley Cup, then Henri Richard is hockey's most successful player; he has 11 Stanley Cup rings — more than any other skater.

By the 1960s goaltending had become a fine art. Jacques Plante (below right) was the first netminder to wear a mask. Plante donned the face covering while a member of the Canadiens before being traded to New York. Glenn Hall, known as "Mr. Goalie" by Chicago fans, developed a unique butterfly stance (below left) that allowed him to drop to the ice to make a save but still remain mobile. Johnny Bower (left) confronts an army of Rangers. Bower's career was stalled in the minor leagues when Leaf coach Punch Imlach called him up to the big team.

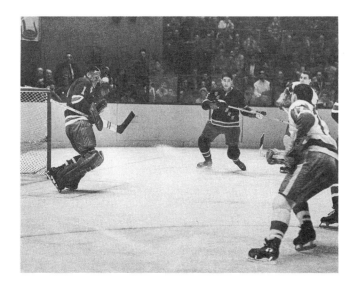

They wrapped up the series with a pair of shutouts (4-0, 2-0) at Chicago Stadium and then met Toronto in the finals.

True champions, the Habs demonstrated that they could play Toronto any way the Leafs chose to operate. "If they wanted to play tough," said center Ralph Backstrom, "we would oblige them. If they wanted to free-wheel, we would be glad to do that. Nothing really bothered us."

This was evident by the final results — 4-2, 2-1, 5-2, 4-0. Just like that; it was over!

For sentimentalists, the most important game of the four was Game Three, April 12, 1960 at Toronto. The Rocket, who had been held scoreless in the previous six playoff games, lit the red light for the last time in his NHL career in the second period for his 82nd playoff goal.

Having won an unprecedented fifth

*Above: Stan Mikita. The Blackhawks'
center worked with his winger, Bobby
Hull, to perfect the curved stick.*

*Right: Rangers captain Andy Bathgate
was a fan favorite and one of the most
exciting players of the early 1960s.*

ster from Regina as the heir apparent to Richard.
While Hicke could fly and fire the puck with
the best of them, he was nowhere near Richard
as a presence, a talent or a battler. In truth, he
was just a cut above a journeyman performer,
an element that would be telling down the
road.

Even without the Rocket, the Canadiens
dominated. At the mid-way mark, they barreled
along with a 22-9-5 record for 49 points and an
eight-point lead over second place Toronto. The
Leafs, looking more like a contender with every
week, came on strong at the end but the Habs
held fast and annexed first place with a two-
point edge over Toronto. Surprisingly, Chicago
was a distant third and Detroit even further
behind in fourth. All signs suggested that Montreal and Toronto would meet in the finals but

straight Stanley Cup, the Canadiens were revered as no other club in history. Toe Blake was
at his pinnacle as a coach and likewise Frank
Selke, Sr. never looked better as a manager of
talent. But nobody had to tell Selke that he
would have his hands full trying to replace the
Rocket.

As expected, Maurice Richard announced
his retirement after the Stanley Cup champagne
was quaffed and nobody demurred. The Rocket
had enough trouble slogging through the 1959-
60 campaign and the fact that he was able to
retire a champion was icing on the cake.

Selke turned to his vast farm system for
help and imported Billy Hicke, a squat speed-

as often is the case when it comes to the playoffs, the signals are wrong.

If nothing else, the wear and tear of so many successive marches to the final rounds would have a debilitating effect on the Canadiens and Rudy Pilous was the first to understand this. Consequently, he devised a strategy that would exploit the Habs' weariness.

The bigger Blackhawks, especially defensemen Jack Evans and Moose Vasko, battered the Canadiens at every turn. Captain Jean Beliveau — anointed to teammate Bernie Geoffrion's dismay — took the brunt of the hitting and his game suffered although it wasn't apparent at first since the Habs took the opener, 6-2 at The Forum.

But the stage was set for a grand upset when Chicago captured the second match, 4-3, with the winning goal being scored by Ed Litzenberger, a former Canadien who had been given to the Blackhawks during the "Help The Poor" movement. Some help!

Game Three evolved as the most pivotal of the series; and most turbulent. Tied at one, the teams played fiercely through 52 minutes and 12 seconds of overtime. With Montreal's Dickie Moore in the penalty box for tripping, ex-Canadien Murray Balfour scored the winner, putting Chicago up two games to one. Furious over the outcome, Canadiens coach Toe Blake dashed on to the ice and accosted referee Dalton McArthur. NHL President Clarence Campbell fined Blake $2,000 for his indiscretion.

Montreal rallied with a 5-2 decision tying the series at two but when the teams returned to The Forum, Glenn Hall posted a brilliant 3-0 shutout and then dispatched the Canadiens 3-0 at Chicago Stadium. Attrition, the Law of Averages and the absence of Maurice Richard all contributed to the Canadiens downfall. Geoffrion had been injured early in the series

and, despite a heroic return in Game Six, he was virtually useless. Pilous' intimidation tactics worked and it would provide a powerful lesson for the Montreal general staff in years to come.

Thus, the Canadiens run of five consecutive Stanley Cups ended and now the question remained: who would be the next champion? Detroit staked a claim by overpowering Toronto in five games setting up a Midwest final between the Red Wings and Blackhawks.

In a way the series was decided in Game One when Detroit's starting goalie Terry Sawchuk was injured and replaced by unpredictable Hank Bassen. Sawchuk was able to play only the first period and Bassen moved in his spot to start the second. Chicago won 3-2

Above: An irresistible force (Rangers defenseman Larry Cahan) collides with an immovable object (Dean Prentice of the Bruins) at Madison Square Garden.

Cannonading Drives!
The slap shot and
curved stick became
part and parcel of the
NHL scene in the early
1960s. Rod Gilbert of
the Rangers (right)
follows through on a
shot against the
Blackhawks. Dennis
Hull (below) lets a blast
go from the blue line

Left: A common sight in the early 1960s— the Leafs walking over another team. Here defenseman Carl Brewer finishes a rush against the Rangers whose goalie, Jacques Plante, is well out of the play. The Leafs won the Cup three years in a row, from 1961-64, and again in 1967.

but Detroit — with Bassen in goal — took the second match, 3-1. But Bassen lost the next game whereupon Sawchuk returned and eked out a 2-1 win.

Despite his bum shoulder Sawchuk returned for the fifth game and was bombed 6-3. There was no way he could play in the sixth, and final, match at Detroit's Olympia. Bassen was shelled 5-1 and the Blackhawks had their first Stanley Cup since the outbreak of World War II.

Judging by their youthful lineup and the flowering of Bobby Hull and Stan Mikita — along with Hall's extraordinary goaltending — the Blackhawks looked good enough on paper to reel off another Stanley Cup or two, or even three.

"We had the personnel," said Hall, "but other factors intervened." Namely, the Maple Leafs and Canadiens. By the start of the 1961-62 season, the NHL had reached a quality level rarely matched before or since. Although other sports were rapidly expanding, big-league hockey remained a coccoon-like six-team league that, if nothing else, was brim full of Grade A performers.

"Even third-liners had to be good," said Rod Gilbert of the Rangers, "because if they weren't, management knew there were plenty more to be had in the minors."

Having lost the Cup to Chicago, the Canadiens began rebuilding. They shocked their fans by sending heroic Doug Harvey and Al Langlois to the Rangers for tough defenseman Lou Fontinato while dealing defenseman Bob Turner to Chicago. Plante was retained in goal although his days were said to be numbered.

In Toronto the Maple Leafs were maturing

according to Punch Imlach's plan. One of the few additions was defenseman Al Arbour who had played on Chicago's Cup-winning club. Chicago would have its hands full keeping pace with the Habs and Leafs.

NHL insiders soon realized that one of the Blackhawks prime problems was their accent on offense—at the expense of defense—and an overall lack of discipline despite Pilous' attempts to keep his players in line. Instead of leading the league, the Hawks were a dismal fourth at the mid-point in the season while the Canadiens and Leafs were running neck-and-neck.

With Doug Harvey successfully filling the

Above: Leaf captain George Armstrong, known as the "Chief," hoists the Stanley Cup at a victory parade in Toronto. Club executive and later team owner, Harold Ballard (right) runs interference.

role of player-coach, the Rangers surprised with their invigorating play, particularly the first line with Andy Bathgate, Dean Prentice and Earl Ingarfield. The Broadway Blueshirts battled Detroit for the fourth and final playoff berth, culminating with a decisive game at Madison Square Garden with a few days left in the season. Early in the game Gordie Howe beat Harvey one-on-one to put Detroit ahead but the Rangers eventually tied the count. The winning goal was scored by Bathgate who beat Bassen on a penalty shot.

The win enabled the Rangers to finish fourth behind Chicago, Toronto and Montreal in that order. Amassing 98 points, the Habs were especially impressive with their 13 point bulge over second place Toronto while Chicago was a full ten points behind the Leafs.

As always, the playoffs were a whole new ball game. After taking a two games to none lead over the Blackhawks, Montreal proceeded to lose the next four straight

Likewise, Toronto jumped ahead of the Rangers by two games in the other semi-final. When the series moved to New York, the Blueshirts were aided by Junior star Rod Gilbert and the two games went to the home team.

Game Five was a classic and belonged to goalie Worsley until he committed a goof with more than four minutes gone in the second overtime. The Gump had made a save and fell back with his neck using the puck as a cushion. Worsley correctly believed that referee Eddie Powers would blow his whistle to suspend play but incorrectly lifted his head after a few seconds, mistakenly thinking the whistle had blown.

It had not, and the long whistle would cost the Rangers the game and the playoffs. When Worsley lifted his head, revealing the rubber, Red Kelly of Toronto cheerfully nudged it in and Toronto won the game, 3-2. The dismayed

Rangers were crushed 7-1 in the sixth and final game.

The Blackhawks-Leafs final took on classical proportions of its own, pitting the flamboyant Hull-Mikita combine against the hard-checking, more workmanlike Leafs paced by Frank Mahovlich and Red Kelly. Toronto went ahead two games to none, then Chicago took the next pair. But the Leafs came on strong with an 8-4 triumph and sewed up the series with a gripping 2-1 win at raucous Chicago Stadium.

If nothing else the decision revealed the strong fibre of Imlach's Leafs, who outchecked the Hawks and the basic character weakness that would betray the Chicagoans throughout the Hull-Mikita decade during which the Hawks would not win another Stanley Cup despite a star-sprinkled roster.

Above: Bob Pulford. The Leaf forward was an important ingredient in the team's Stanley Cup success.

Left: Chicago's dynamic duo through the middle 1960s was Bobby Hull (right) and his brother Dennis. Fans argued about who's slap shot was harder.

Toronto would win two more Stanley Cups — in 1963 and 1964 — under Imlach, matching the accomplishment of Hap Day in 1947, 1948, 1949. The 1962-63 Leafs were analogous to the 1947-48 club. Toronto finished first, nipping Chicago by a single point, and featured center ice strength — Bob Pulford, Red Kelly, Dave Keon — reminiscent of Apps, Bentley and Kennedy.

Imlach gained revenge over his opposite, Toe Blake, with a four games to one playoff rout in the semi-finals while Detroit bested Chicago in six games. The final was a waltz for Toronto; only five games were required to dispose of the Red Wings, and this despite the fact that Mahovlich failed to score throughout the playoffs.

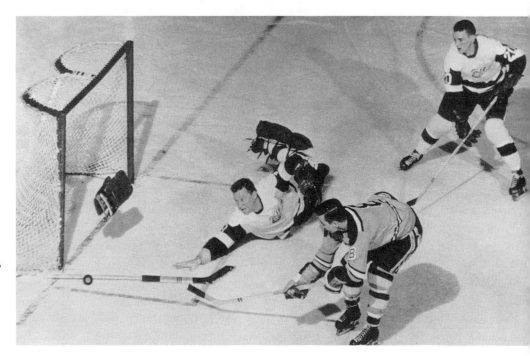

Right: Detroit goalie Hank Bassen throws everything but the kitchen sink at Boston's Wayne Connelly to keep him from scoring.

Below: Detroit's Bill Gadsby.

The Canadiens high command did not have to be told that the balance of NHL power had dramatically shifted to Toronto, nor that the nucleus of their five-Cup teams could still gen-erate enough power. With that in mind, the Habs began dismantling their once-vaunted lineup.

Plante, who had become the most innova-tive and one of the most competent goalies of all time, was dealt to the Rangers along with Phil Goyette and Don Marshall. Montreal re-ceived Worsley and forwards Dave Balon and Leon Rochefort.

Determined not to be intimidated, the Canadiens also secured John Ferguson, a ham-fisted minor leaguer who also scored a few goals for the Cleveland Barons. Ferguson was explicitly told to ride shotgun for captain Jean Beliveau but he did more than that.

"They wanted me to be sure that nobody took any liberties with Jean," says Ferguson, "and that was fine with me. But I don't think they expected me to score the way I did. That's one reason why I was able to hang around the NHL as long as I did."

Although nobody made much of it at the time, Ferguson became the NHL's first genuine "enforcer" and would continue to do so through ve Stanley Cups. Other teams took due note of Fergie's value and, in time, the age of the ockey cop was upon the NHL.

The Canadiens were not the only ones bent n shakeup. The Blackhawks bosses were emi-ently dismayed by the club's failure to win nother championship after the 1961 triumph nd Rudy Pilous was made the fall guy. He vas replaced as coach by Billy Reay before the 963-64 season

Montreal's dressing room was conspicu-usly more harmonious without Plante. The Canadiens led the pack with 85 points while Reay nudged the Hawks into second only a oint behind. Toronto was third with 78 but hat never bothered Imlach whose chief con-ern was revving his club up at playoff time; vhich he did. Martinet though he was, Imlach till was able to squeeze maximum ability out f his skaters at the right time.

The Leafs eliminated Montreal in a seven-ame semi-final. Detroit and Chicago also went he limit and, this time, Sawchuk beat Hall 4-2 n Game Seven.

Sentimentality crept into the finals with an nusual amount of schmaltz coating stories. he media realized that this might be the last pportunity for two grand warriors, Gordie Iowe and Bill Gadsby, to grab the golden ring. Iowe had played on many Cup teams but Gadsby, who would play 20 full NHL seasons, ever sipped the champagne.

Now, it seemed that Gadsby would have is dream realized. The Wings took a three ames to two series lead and tied Toronto 3-3 hrough regulation time in Game Six. One goal vould do it for Detroit.

It was not meant to be, for Gadsby or his eammates. Bob Baun, the Toronto defenseman vho earlier suffered a broken leg, had his in-ury frozen and took the ice in the overtime. At :43 of the extra session Baun took a pass from

Above: Detroit's distinguished captain, Alex Delvecchio, who played his first game during the 1950 season and his last in 1974. Delvecchio played in 1549 games during his career and scored 1249 total points.

Pulford and beat Sawchuk. In the seventh game Johnny Bower blanked the Red Wings 4-0. Imlach had a Stanley Cup hat trick.

The celebrations notwithstanding, several of the Maple Leaf players understood that the latest Toronto dynasty had come to an end although it had nothing to do with talent or age. Imlach's robo-cop style had terribly bruised the psyches of some players — Frank Mahovlich and Carl Brewer, to name two — and offended others. Disenchantment led to dissension and it was the latter element which scuttled the Leafs' ship as much as anything.

As the 1965-66 season approached, NHL owners were confronted with an issue that had vexed them for years but had now taken on new meaning. Attendance was superb through-

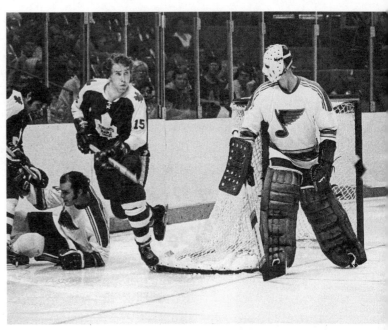

Above: Four expansion uniforms, as modelled by the netminders. Clockwise from the top left: Roger Crozier of the Buffalo Sabres, Ernie Wakely of the St. Louis Blues, Bernie Parent of the Philadelphia Flyers.

out the six-team league and several governors were tickled with that. But a couple of young turks, led by the Rangers president Bill Jennings, believed that the NHL could be even more successful if it expanded beyond its half-dozen members. Where once the conservatives had

ruled the roost, now the expansionists were being heard — loud and clear.

Jennings exuded confidence in hockey's drawing power and finally convinced his peers that it would be to their monetary advantage to add no less than six new franchises and that the NHL would be able to absorb the ballooning to twelve clubs.

While the back room dickering went on Imlach's Maple Leafs somehow managed to ınite one more time and won the 1967 Stanley Cup, the last such championship held in the six-team league.

Following the playoffs, plans were laid to ıncorporate the Oakland Seals, Los Angeles Kings, St.Louis Blues, Minnesota North Stars, Philadelphia Flyers and Pittsburgh Penguins ınto the expanded NHL. The cost of a franchise was $2 million and for the money the new ïeams obtained a handful of older stars, some ɔotential aces and most minor leaguers who had languished in the American Hockey League.

Some teams got lucky. The Flyers, for one, drafted goalie Bernie Parent from the Boston Bruins and, as luck would have it, Parent became a Hall of Famer and the cornerstone of Philadelphia's Stanley Cup championship teams in 1974 and 1975.

The Seals were not so lucky. Management believed that it was imperative to collect as many "name" NHLers as possible so as to im-

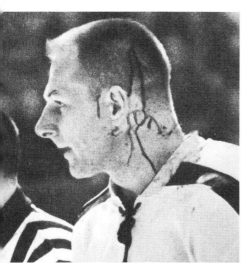

The menacing use of hockey sticks as weapons has always been a part of the game's dark side. Here, Eddie Shack of the Boston Bruins (left) trades blows with Larry Zeidel (right) of the Phila-delphia Flyers during a bloody 1968 match.

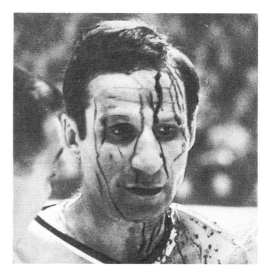

mediately attract fans in an admitted non-hockey city. Players such as Bob Baun and Gerry Ehman had NHL names, to be sure, but their talent level was less than expected and attendance was low. It was a portent of things to come.

It was decided that all the expansion teams should be placed in the newly-created West Division. If nothing else, the race was so tight that playoff positions were not decided until the final weekend in which Philadelphia finished on top.

"We weren't that strong a team," said Larry Zeidel who played defense for the Flyers, "but we were a TEAM and we gave one hundred percent every night. When we beat the Canadiens, everyone in the league took notice."

Unobtrusive at first, the Blues rallied in the stretch under coach Scott Bowman and then added former Canadiens stars Doug Harvey and Dickie Moore for the playoffs. What's more, St.Louis had drafted goalie Glenn Hall from Chicago and Mister Goalie performed extraordinary feats as the Blues swept past Philadel-

phia and went all the way to the Stanley Cup finals where they collided with Montreal.

Veteran fans accustomed to the six-team NHL were appalled by the low quality of play in the finals. The Canadiens often appeared to be toying with the Blues and swept through the series in four games. It was a Stanley Cup final virtually bereft of excitement — except for the citizens of St.Louis.

The Blues unearthed another crowd-pleaser in Gordon "Red" Berenson, a center who had previously been rejected by both the Rangers and Canadiens. In St.Louis, Berenson not only found a home but achieved a stardom that had eluded him throughout his professional career. In one game against the Flyers he totalled no less than six goals and became the toast of St.Louis Arena.

Expansion succeeded in most cities, but not all. In Oakland, the Seals suffered endless ownership problems the likes of which would eventually doom the franchise. Similar fiscal aches bedeviled the Penguins but, somehow, the franchise remained afloat. St.Louis, Philadelphia, Minnesota and Los Angeles gradually developed enough of a fan base — or stability of ownership — to stay in business and work toward turning a profit.

Gradually, heroes were developed in all six expansion cities. In addition to Berenson and Hall, the Blues were enamored with the turbulent Plager Brothers, Barclay and Bob, who hit everything in sight and gave the St.Louis back line the kind of protection few NHL clubs received. Rangers reject Cesare "Hail Caesar" Maniago became the darling of Minnesota with his acrobatic kick saves between the pipes while a former minor league trainer named Les Binkley turned hero as the Penguins surprisingly agile goaltender.

"I beat the Bruins 1-0 one night in Boston Garden," Binkley recalled, "and the franchise seemed to pick up right from there."

One expansion player with promise never got to fulfill his potential. Bill Masterton, a North Stars teammate of Maniago, led a rush into enemy territory on the night of January 13, 1968 at Met Center in Bloomington. Oakland defensemen Larry "Hank" Cahan and Ron Harris, both harsh bodycheckers, converged on Masterton and delivered a clean, double-check, sending the Minnesota forward flipping backward through the air. When Masterton hit his head on the ice, players, fans and officials realized that he was seriously hurt.

Rushed to a hospital, Masterton never regained consciousness despite 30 hours of intensive efforts by the surgeons to save his life. On the morning of January 15, he died of massive internal brain damage.

The tragedy coursed through the entire league like rushing water from a broken dam. Player after player was enveloped in the negative fallout with the result that several top-of-the-line stickhandlers, led by Chicago's Stan Mikita, announced that hereafter they would wear protective headgear to prevent a similar injury.

At first only a handful of skaters adopted the headgear but, gradually, more and more took to wearing them as the helmets were perfected by manufacturers. The NHL did its part

Below: Orr and Espo — the end of the 1960's saw a revitalized Boston Bruin team, built around the nucleus Bobby Orr (left) and Phil Esposito.

Opposite Page: Orr revolutionized the role of defenseman in 1966-67 when he made his debut. Orr could play defensive hockey, as this shot illustrates, but he also organized the Bruin offense in a manner never seen before.

to honor the deceased player by striking a new award, the Bill Masterton Memorial Trophy, for the player who exemplifies the finer traits of the game and emulates the behavior of Masterton.

As a hockey team, the North Stars were no great shakes but the West (expansion) Division did get its jollies from the Blues in 1968-69. Bowman had acquired Jacques Plante to alternate in goal with Glenn Hall and this tandem would prove to be one of the best — not to mention oldest — the pro game has seen. Together, they won The Vezina Trophy while the Blues finished a full 19 points ahead of second place Oakland.

The East (established) Division was highlighted by a keen race between the Canadiens and a resurgent Bruins team led by Robert Gordon (Bobby) Orr, a true marvel on skates. Although officially called a defenseman, Orr used his exceptional skating ability to spear-head end-to-end rushes that placed him on the attack as much as — if not more — than he was on defense.

After a rookie year in which his Bruins finished last (1966-67), Orr and the Bruins began feeling their oats with expansion. Bobby was aided in large part by a one-sided trade with Chicago that brought Phil Esposito, Fred Stanfield and Ken Hodge to Boston. Orr and Esposito would make beautiful music together for many years while igniting a revival of hockey interest in Beantown.

An average forward when he toiled for the Blackhawks, Esposito set a point record of 126 as well as a new assist mark of 77 in 1968-69. The Bruins became the first NHL team ever to score more than 300 goals. They hit for a total of 303 and that alone was enough to list them as a good bet to unseat the Canadiens as Stanley Cup champions.

With a late rush, the Habs edged the "Big

Right: Glenn Hall sparkled during his final years in the league with the expansion St. Louis Blues. Here Hall guards against a Los Angeles King attacker. The defenseman to his right is Al Arbour, who would later coach another expansion team (the New York Islanders) to four Stanley Cup championships.

Left: The Philadelphia Flyers moved boldly from the onset, first snatching future Hall-of-Famer Bernie Parent from the Boston Bruins and then signing francise player Bobby Clarke, seen here shaking hands with club owner Ed Snider while aide John Brogan looks on.

Bad Bruins" — they got that name because they intimidated the opposition as few teams ever had — on the final weekend of the campaign. They met again in the semi-finals and while the Bruins gave the Canadiens fits (three games were decided in sudden-death), Montreal came out on top, four games to two.

Meanwhile, the Blues fought their way to the finals for the second straight year and actually made the Canadiens work hard to beat them but win the Habs did in four straight for a successful defense of the Cup.

If nothing else, the Blues game performance offered some evidence that the expansion teams were improving; maybe not by leaps and bounds but certainly perceptibly enough to please the owners who pushed for doubling the league's size. A few of the more ambitious governors suggested that it was time to consider even further expansion and they cited the glut of new arenas which were popping up all over the country. One of them was in Nassau County (Long Island), New York, an hour's drive from Madison Square Garden and another, surprise of surprises, was located in the Deep South. Atlanta, Georgia, to be precise, not to mention Buffalo and Vancouver.

World class hockey also was spreading its influence in other parts of the globe. With each year after World War II, the Soviet Union studied, applied and improved its hockey program to a point where the Russian stickhandlers routinely won games on an international level, although not against NHL opponents.

The Soviets craved competition with the West while the NHL leaders eyed the Russians with a mixture of skepticism and curiosity, with the latter gradually overwhelming the former.

As these forces built in size, they would generate startling developments in the 1970s, some which would dwarf the growth of hockey in the previous decade.

CHAPTER EIGHT

The NHL Goes to War — Again

As soon as it had become apparent that expansion teams such as the Blues and Flyers could make a buck, other promoters hustled to get on the NHL bandwagon. Applications to join the league came from all points of the compass but among the most vigorous prospective owners were those in Vancouver and Buffalo.

Each had attempted to get in the first time around but because of a combination of league politics and a desire for larger cities, both were rejected. Undaunted, they continued lobbying and finally got an attentive NHL ear by the time the 1969-70 season was underway. The governors agreed that each city had a virtue as a future lodge member and it was agreed that Vancouver and Buffalo would gain admission for the 1970-71 schedule.

In the meantime rivalries began to flourish between the established clubs and the new-comers. As early as 1967-68 the Flyers and Bruins were at each other's throats and one clash erupted into a vicious stick fight between Philadelphia's Larry Zeidel and Eddie Shack of the Bruins. There was no love lost between the

Canadiens and Blues, especially after St.Louis lost eight straight playoff games to the champs

Yet another rivalry developed rather unexpectedly during a pre-season exhibition game between the Bruins and Blues, one which would have tragic long-term overtones. Boston defenseman Ted Green had, over the years, earned a reputation as one of the toughest most intense players in the business; one who would have little compunction about jamming his stick into an enemy's stomach, as Phil Goyette once learned.

Few skaters in their right mind would challenge Green but, occasionally, another tough guy such as John Ferguson, or a young whippersnapper would go head-to-head with "Terrible Ted." The Blues' youthful Wayne Maki did so on this occasion. Sticks rose but instead of the traditional dropping of the lumber and then the punching interlude, neither player let go of his weapon. Instead, they began swinging at one another with Maki whacking the Bruin right in the head. Green fell to the ice, his brain embedded with chips from his skull. Two

a two-man axis — Phil Esposito and Bobby Orr. The latter had grown to Promethian proportions. Experts throughout the league tabbed him the best player of the decade and some even suggested that he would rank among the greatest performers the NHL has known. Certainly, his efforts at the start of the new decade suggested that all of the above were true. Although he was listed as a defenseman, Orr won the league scoring title (33-87-120), the Hart Trophy and the Norris Trophy, a parlay no defenseman ever equalled.

Nevertheless, the Bruins were not the league's best team, point-wise, over the regular schedule. The Blackhawks, reinforced in goal with rookie Tony Esposito's exceptional goaltending, still were able to squeeze world-class efforts out of Bobby Hull and Stan Mikita while understudies such as Pit Martin and defenseman Pat Stapleton enjoyed career years. Chicago finished first (45-22-9), an event which was a bit less surprising than the failure of the

operations were necessary to save his life but even then, Green was left with his left side paralyzed. To many longtime observers, the Green-Maki affair was reminiscent of the Gordie Howe-Ted Kennedy incident and Ace Bailey-Eddie Shore of an earlier era.

After a delicate operation in which a plate was inserted in his head, Green gradually recovered but was unable to play hockey for the remainder of the season. Maki would return to NHL activity but his life proved even more tragic than Green's. Maki died of a brain tumour in 1974.

The 1969-70 season was highlighted by Boston's resurgence as a hockey power. Not since the pre-war days of the Kraut Line, Frankie Brimsek and Bill Cowley had the Bruins iced so formidable a team. They had solid goaltending from Gerry Cheevers and Eddie Johnston, an experienced defense, well-balanced scoring and ideal role players such as Derek "Turk" Sanderson, a center who could score and also was one of the league's top penalty-killers.

But most of all, the Bruins revolved around

One of the tragic clashes of the early expansion era involved Wayne Maki (14) of the St. Louis Blues and Ted Green of the Bruins. In an exhibition game before the 1969 season the two got into a vicious stick fight. Maki's blow to Green's head fractured the Bruins' skull, nearly ending his life.

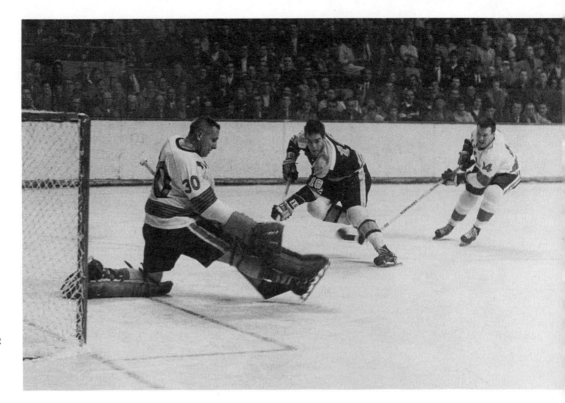

Right: Boston's Derek Sanderson breaks in alone on Pittsburgh's Les Binkley.

defending champion Canadiens to even make the playoffs.

Montreal's workhorses, Jean Beliveau and John Ferguson, suffered from the wear and tear of overwork and dissension gripped the team that once was filled with elan. The Habs approached the final game of the season with a two-point lead over the Rangers and were five ahead in the goals scored column. But if the Canadiens lost and the Rangers won — *and* the Rangers could make up the goal deficit, New York and not Montreal would qualify for the playoffs.

In a bizarre scenario, the Rangers wasted an uninterested Detroit team, 9-5, at Madison Square Garden whereas the Blackhawks destroyed the Canadiens, 10-2 in Chicago and, thus, the champs were out, the New Yorkers were in and the highway to The Stanley Cup was wide open.

Any designs the Blackhawks may have conjured up about a championship were unraveled in the East semi-finals by the Bruins.

Boston forwards picked apart the Chicago defense and had no trouble solving Tony Esposito. One, two, three, four and the Hawks were gone.

Scott Bowman's Blues once again dominated the West (expansion) Division playoffs and reached the finals for the third straight season; a feat that stirred hockey interest in St. Louis to a frenzy. It was hoped that the Glenn Hall-Jacques Plante goaltending combine could somehow thwart the Bruins but it was not to be and for the third time in three years, St. Louis was ousted without winning a single game.

To Boston fans, the Cup-winning goal was symbolically perfect. In the overtime period of Game Four, the incomparable Orr swept the puck past Hall and almost simultaneously was tripped by defenseman Noel Picard. Orr took flight — his body actually resembled Superman gliding through the air — as a result of the trip and was horizontal, about two feet above the ice, when the red light flashed.

"Bobby was the God of Boston hockey at

he time," said Ed Westfall, a teammate and key cog in the Bruins machine, "so it was only right that he got the winner."

Orr not only captivated Beantown, his charisma carried throughout the league and helped bolster the expansion process. In 1970-71 both Buffalo and Vancouver made their respective NHL debuts. The Sabres were created by George "Punch" Imlach of Maple Leaf fame while the Canucks were organized by Bud Poile who had been the original general manager of the Flyers in 1967.

Imlach caught a break when he was allowed to select first in the expansion draft and picked a French-Canadian speedster, Gil Perreault, who ultimately would be a Hall of Famer. By contrast, Poile chose Dale Tallon, a promising defenseman who never quite fulfilled his notices and wound up behind a mi-

crophone analyzing hockey for SportsChannel Chicago.

Expansion had further diluted NHL talent and when Imlach convened his Sabres at training camp, he put it bluntly: "You're here because nobody else wanted you. As far as I'm concerned, you don't have the ability to play for any other NHL team, or you wouldn't be here. But we'll even things up — with dedication, more hustle and being in better shape. We'll be competitive from our first game."

Expansion teams had to dig harder for talent and often resorted to players who were ignored by the established clubs. For example, the Flyers took a gamble on a gap-toothed diabetic from Flin Flon, Manitoba named Bobby

Below: The great Bobby Orr in mid-flight after scoring the Stanley Cup winning goal in 1970.

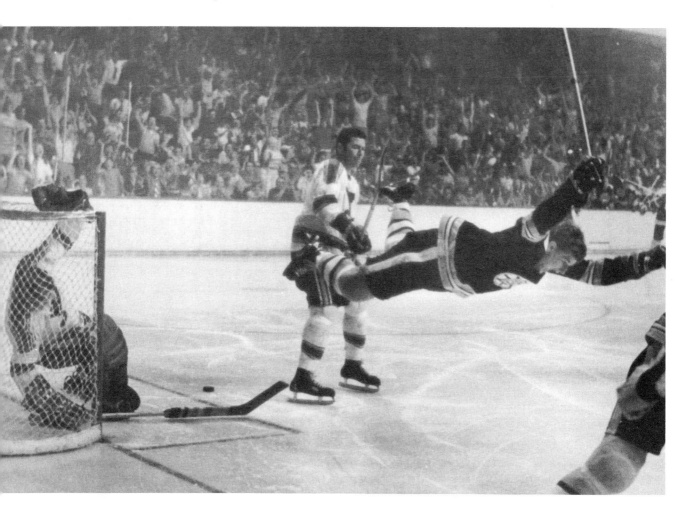

Two new young stars: Right: Gilbert Perreault with Buffalo Sabres coach "Punch" Imlach celebrating Perreault's 35th goal in his rookie season on March 18, 1971 — breaking a 45-year-old record set by Nels Stewart in 1925.

Below: Philadelphia Flyers Bobby Clarke, one of the grittiest, most intense players in NHL history.

Clarke. Most teams were quite willing to pass on Clarke because of his diabetes alone. Others figured that he couldn't cut it on ability but Bobby proved an extraordinary worker who in time would become the most important forward in Philadelphia hockey history.

The Bruins had no talent concerns. Their nucleus was intact and even Ted Green had miraculously made it back to the Boston lineup on defense, although he was forced to wear an ugly black helmet for protection. The Orr-Esposito tandem was enough to inspire critics to predict a spate of Stanley Cups for the Hub sextet and some even thought they could match the Canadiens record of five straight titles.

But it was not to be because the Bruins were afflicted with the same problem — indiscipline — that overcome the Blackhawks a decade earlier. The Bruins freewheeled on and off the ice, which made wonderful newspaper copy but hardly provided the glue necessary when the playoff chips were down.

And they were down in the 1971 Cup round. A Montreal club that appeared to have no business on the same rink with Boston unceremoniously dethroned the Bruins in a seven game series. Orr and Esposito were bumped from center stage by Ken Dryden, a former Cornell University goaltender, who had only six games of NHL experience before being

rust on the Stanley Cup firing line. Unper-
urbed, Dryden weathered a couple of bumpy
ames, then settled down and thoroughly frus-
ated the defending champions. His 4-2 win in
ame Seven left the Bruins shaking their heads.

"Dryden was un-real," said Esposito. "He
as the series." Having disposed of Boston, the
anadiens sped all the way to the finals where
ey engaged the Blackhawks in another seven-
ame thriller. The finale took place at Chicago
tadium, May 18, 1971, and this, too, was a
assic. The Hawks nursed a 2-0 lead into the
cond period when Jacques Lemaire beat Tony
sposito with a stoppable long shot. Shortly

thereafter, Henri Richard tied the score and the
Pocket Rocket got the winner in the third period.

The thoroughly unlikely Stanley Cup vic-
tory was made even more unusual by the
Canadiens' players attitude toward coach Al
MacNeil. Team captain Henri Richard called
MacNeil one of the worst coaches he ever played
for and, within a month of the Cup celebration,

*Below: The Cinderella story of the 1970s — Ken
Dryden emerged from Cornell University late in the
1970-71 season to lead the Candiens to a Stanley
Cup victory. In his 8 year career, Dryden won the
Vezina 5 times and the Stanley Cup 5 times.*

Right: Chicago's ace goalie Tony Esposito sparkled in the 1970-71 season, recording a 35/14/6 win, loss and tie record, but a long floater from Montreal's Jacques Lemaire (below, shown here playing against the Rangers) in the 7th game of the Stanley Cup finals deflated the Blackhawks' championship hopes.

MacNeil quit the Habs. His replacement, Scott Bowman, would rival Toe Blake and Dick Irvin on the Montreal coaching greatness scale.

Winning another Cup would not be easy for Bowman at first. With Beliveau rapidly showing his age, the Habs strove to integrate new faces into the lineup but this came at the expense of quality. Meanwhile, the Rangers were revived on Broadway thanks, in large part, to the scoring proclivity of the "GAG" (Goal A Game) Line featuring Rod Gilbert on right wing, Jean Ratelle at center and Vic Hadfield not to mention the goaltending duet of Ed Giacomin and Gilles Villemure.

Stung by their early playoff exit, the Bruins also were prepared to atone for their debacle with basically the same roster but a new attitude. That was reflected in the standings. With 54 wins, only 13 losses and 11 ties, the Bruins finished first overall and added individual trophies as well. Phil Esposito copped the Art Ross Trophy as leading scorer while Orr took the Hart and Norris Trophies.

Two questions were uppermost in the minds of fans; 1. Could the Canadiens pull off another miracle playoff win? 2. Would the Bruins vindicate themselves as they had in 1970?

Answer 1 was provided soon enough. The Rangers knocked off Montreal in six games

Above: Oh, brother! Phil Esposito is parked in his characteristic spot — the opposing team's goal crease. On this occasion he tries to bat the puck in against his brother, Tony. Below: "Espo" on a solo dash.

and nothing Ken Dryden nor Scott Bowman could devise would thwart the New Yorkers. Answer 2 required more time. Boston danced past Toronto and St.Louis entering the finals with terrifyingly strong momentum. The Rangers had what g.m. Emile Francis called "the best team since I've been running the club."

Unfortunately, New York lost Ratelle through a late season injury and fell behind three games to one before rallying for an unexpected victory at Boston Garden to trim the Bruins lead to three games to two.

The Rangers had hoped to tie the series at home but simply could not contain the peripatetic Orr who danced around New York's Bruce MacGregor at the right point and homed in on net for the first — and winning — goal. The

Rangers gave it their best shot but they simply didn't have the armament to match Boston's front line. The final score was 3-0 Bruins.

While the Stanley Cup finals were in full swing a number of off-ice developments were unfolding which would have long-term ramifications for the Game. In California, a group of entrepreneurs led by attorney Gary Davidson decided to exploit the hockey boom by creating a major league of their own. Throughout the spring and summer, Davidson & Co. plotted ways and means of luring top names to their circuit.

On another front, Alan Eagleson, an agent who doubled as executive director of the NHL Players' Association, began negotiating with Soviet hockey authorities with an eye toward staging an eight-game series between an NHL All-Star team and the cream of Russian hockey.

Both groups pushed ahead during the summer and by August the NHLers were training for the tournament which would open with four contests in Canada and conclude with four more in the Soviet Union. It would prove to be a truly momentous event, particularly in view of the gains made by the Russians.

The opening game was scheduled for September 2, 1972, at the Forum in Montreal. Never in the history of hockey has more attention been riveted on one game and one series. In Canada more than twelve million people focused on their television sets when the puck was dropped for the opening face-off.

When Phil Esposito of Team Canada scored after only thirty seconds of play the capacity crowd fully expected a rout. A goal by Paul Henderson six minutes later merely confirmed their suspicions. But the Soviets rallied to tie the score, 2-2, before the period had ended. The Russians scored twice in the second period and three times in the third, but Team Canada could manage only one more goal. The final score

was 7-3 for the Soviets, and all of Canada was in shock. "Two marks to the Soviets," shouted an editorial in the Toronto Sun.

The Dominion collectively breathed a sigh of relief after game two, played at Maple Leaf Gardens in Toronto. With the score 2-1 for Team Canada in the third period and the Russians threatening, the NHL stars broke the game open and won it, 4-1.

Game three, played at Winnipeg, ended in a 4-4 tie, but several meaningful insights were percolating among the experts. Most significant was the fact that the Russians were, at the very least, a match for the NHL skaters. Furthermore, the Soviets were in better condition and were not likely to be routed in any given game of the series. The hopes for an unequivocal rout administered by the NHL team were now completely dashed. "The only thing I don't like about this series," said Eagleson, "are the games!"

Game four, played at Vancouver, was an utter humiliation for the Canadians. The final score was 5-3 for the Russians, but their mastery of several aspects of the game distressed the players even more than the score. "The Soviets shoot quicker than NHL players," said goalie Ken Dryden. "They start moving around a defenseman and while an NHL player would do the job and then shoot, the Soviets seem to release their shots while they're moving around the defensemen."

The Russians demonstrated beyond shadow of a doubt that they could defend as well as score and, furthermore, the goaltending of Vladislav Tretiak was impeccable. Even worse for Team Canada, the audience at the Pacific Coliseum turned against them. Harry Sinden the Canadian coach, would have to huddle with his brain trust to devise new strategies for the four-game set coming up in the Soviet Union. "I knew the Canadian pride was hurt," said Sinden

Team Canada's Paul Henderson (left) scored the winning goal against the USSR in the final seconds. Two of the Soviet stars were Yuri Liapkin (above left) and Boris Mikhailov (above right).

Hockey was our game and now someone was trying to take it away from us."

Game five was played at Moscow and, from all appearances, Team Canada seemed en route to victory. The Canadians scored the first three goals of the game and led, 4-1, with only eleven minutes remaining, when suddenly the Russians struck back with four straight goals. The final score was 5-4 for the hosts. "The Russians," said Sinden, "play this game as though there were no scoreboard, no ups and downs. No team in the NHL would have played the way they did in the last ten minutes, down 4-1 and still skating and shooting and passing the puck the same way they did in the first period."

A desperate Canadian team showed up for game six at Moscow and proved its mettle. Trailing 1-0, the Canadians counterattacked for three consecutive goals and held on for a 3-2 victory. The seventh game was another one right out of a Hollywood script. With the score tied, 3-3, late in the third period Paul Henderson pushed the puck through the legs of a Russian defender. "I got a bit of a break," said Henderson. "The puck hit his skate, deflected it

to his right, and that gave me the chance I needed. While he was looking for it I moved around him. I had pretty good balance and let the shot go." The shot beat Soviet goalie Vladislav Tretiak at 17:54, and the Canadians skated off the ice with a 4-3 triumph. The series was tied at three games apiece with one tie.

The eighth and final game was played on September 28, 1972, at Moscow. In the opinion of many experts it was one of the greatest games ever played. Certainly, millions of Canadians felt that way — after it was all over. Obviously, it was important to the Soviets as well, since they allegedly resorted to a number of ploys to keep the Canadians on edge.

"The Soviets did everything they could to intimidate us," said Phil Esposito, Team Canada's crack center. "They tried to aggravate us off the ice but the fact that we could intimidate them on the ice won it for us."

For two periods the Russians seemed to have the Canadians intimidated. The Soviets nursed a 5-3 lead into the third period when Team Canada fought back. They tied the score with fewer than eight minutes remaining. They won it when Paul Henderson shot the puck at Tretiak and into the net. "It was," said Frank Orr of the *Toronto Sun*, "the most famous goal in the history of hockey."

When the final score (6-5) was posted, all of Canada was delirious with joy. In some ways the reverberations are still being felt to this day.

The same can be said for the World Hockey Association. Although NHL moguls remained militantly skeptical about the proposed league, Davidson moved relentlessly ahead, pursuing some of the NHL's finest talent, stars such as Bobby Hull, Bernie Parent, and Derek Sanderson. They didn't get every man they went after, but the WHA made quite a dent in the rosters of many an NHL club.

The WHA was sprinkled with a few NHL stars that first season, but mostly was loaded with journeymen and minor leaguers. These mediocre players were collecting paychecks far in excess of their worth.

What the WHA lacked in talent it tried t make up for in rule changes. Among them – allowing player-coaches, playing a 10-minut sudden-death overtime period in tie games, n "third man in" rule in a fight and no icing th puck on a penalty unless the player doing s carries the puck over the blue line.

The WHA also persuaded both CBS an the Canadian Broadcasting Company to carr some of the games, a major step for a bran new league. Unfortunately, the WHA lost it television contract after that first year.

The Boston-based New England Whaler won the AVCO World Trophy in 1973 to be come the WHA champions by defeating th Hull-led Jets in five games. As expected, th Golden Jet was the league's most valuabl player although he failed to win the scorin title, which went to Andrew Lacroix of th Philadelphia Blazers.

While the first WHA season could b

Right: The 1972 hockey series between Canada's best players — the cream of the NHL — and the Soviet All-Stars was supposed to be a walk for the Canadians. In the end it came down to the final 38 seconds of the last game for Team Canada to win. Shown celebrating are (left to right) Phil Esposito, Dennis Hull, Serge Savard and Bobby Clarke. The Soviet teams incredible goaltender, Vladislav Tretiak, stares down in dejection.

Left: The World Hockey Association was born in a New York hotel room in 1971. Most NHL observers refused to take the league seriously until Bobby Hull (below right) signed with the Winnipeg Jets. Gary L. Davidson (below left) was the brash mastermind of the league — and its president.

ermed a success for the Whalers and a few thers (notably the Minnesota Fighting Saints nd the Cleveland Crusaders) quite a number f the outfits were on very shaky footing. The hiladelphia Blazers, who had paid a vast sum o Derek Sanderson, lost him early in the cam- aign. Bernie Parent also left the Blazers dur- ng the play-offs. Both Sanderson and Parent eturned to the NHL. The Ottawa Nationals

moved to Toronto and the Blazers to Vancou- ver, respectively. In those cities, the new teams attempted to go head-on in competition for fan support, in the same arenas, with teams from the older circuit.

The WHA's belief that there were plenty of lucrative hockey markets to be milked was ac- cepted in part by the NHL which embraced the New York Islanders (Nassau County) and At-

Say it ain't so!
After 25 years in a Red Wings uniform, Gordie Howe (right) was lured away in 1973 by the Houston Aeros. Howe played 4 seasons with the Aeros and another two with New England, before returning to the NHL with the Whalers when the two leagues merged in 1979.

Below: Two other NHL stalwarts to make the jump to the WHL were Pat Stapleton (left) and Ted Green.

nta Flames for the 1972-73 season. The move to the Deep South was both creative and daring. With ex-Canadien Bernie Geoffrion as Georgia's hockey evangelist, the ice game caught on almost immediately in the peach tree state and soon after a minor league club sprouted in Macon, Georgia. It's name: the Macon Whoopees!

Its rosters depleted by WHA raids, the NHL mucked along and still drew hefty gates up and down the line. But Boston suffered grievously from its defections and was hardly a playoff factor as the Canadiens topped the league standings and defeated Chicago four games to two for the 1973 Stanley Cup.

NHL moguls had hoped the WHA would have expired by 1973-74 but every time one club folded, the new league managed to find an angel and a site for a a replacement. As a result, NHL rosters continued to be stripped of talent with such notable names as Gordie Howe —

along with sons Mark and Marty — Gerry Cheevers and Ted Green gracing the upstart WHA.

Desperate for replacements, the NHL frequently stooped to hiring less-talented tough players who would just as soon play goon hockey as they would go the artistic route. The Flyers were able to do both. General manager Keith Allen put together a squad of gifted players such as Bernie Parent, Bob Clarke, Bill Barber and Ed Van Impe and sprinkled the roster with just enough tough guys like Dave "Hammer" Schultz, Andre (Moose) Dupont and Bob "Hound" Kelly. With the encouragement of Fred "The Fog" Shero behind the bench, the Flyers terrorized the league and earned the nickname, The Broad Street Bullies. They also won enough hockey games to enter the 1974 playoffs a distant but not altogether hopeless choice to become the first expansion team to win a Stanley Cup.

Left: In the middle 1970s the NHL was dominated by the Philadelphia Flyers. Known collectively as the "Broad Street Bullies," the Flyers shut down more talented teams by playing an aggressive, often ugly brand of grinding hockey. Here, they clear the benches against the Rangers. Note in the center of the melee, goaltender Bernie Parent laying a beating on an unlucky Ranger skater— even the Flyer creasemen mixed it up.

A good barometer of the Flyers ability was provided in the playoff against the Rangers. The more experienced New Yorkers were pulverized by Clarke and his sluggers and exited after seven games. When the Flyers reached the finals they were a much more formidable opponent than any expansion team and took on the Bruins — league leaders over the regular campaign — without blinking an eye.

To the astonishment of just about everyone, the Flyers fought their way to a three games to two lead and them bumped off the Bruins, 1-0, in Game Six on the strength of Rick MacLeish's first period goal. Bedlam overcame The City of Brotherly Love and the Flyers were then firmly established as one of the strongest of franchises.

Any suggestion that the 1974 triumph was a fluke was dispelled a year later when Philadelphia finished with the best regular schedule record (51-18-11), stormed to the finals and this

time ousted another expansion club, the Buffalo Sabres.

That the Flyers often bludgeoned their way to victory caused considerable consternation among hockey purists. Dave Schultz, Bob Kelly and Moose Dupont frequently were criticized by the media and NHL President Clarence Campbell was hard-pressed to defend their actions. Goon hockey was at its peak if for no other reason than the Flyers twin Stanley Cup championships and their ability to outdraw any other club in the league.

The Philadelphia juggernaut continued to roll in 1975-76 although Scott Bowman had now sculpted an impressive roster in Montreal. Ken Dryden had fulfilled his notices in goal while defense headed by Serge Savard and Guy Lapointe ranked as the league's best. Guy

In addition to the grit of Bobby Clarke and the brawn of the team's numerous pugilists, the Flyers also possessed some talented personnel. Among them, second goalie Doug Favell (above), veteran skater Ed Van Impe (opposite page at top), and — perhaps most important of all — good luck charm vocalist, Kate Smith, shown here belting out "God Bless America" on May 19, 1974 before the Flyers' Cup clinching 1-0 victory over the Boston Bruins.

hung on and, by 1976-77, was bleeding the NHL white. Several NHL leaders, led by Ed Snider and Bill Jennings proposed that a merger take place or some sort of accommodation to end the inter-league war but conservative elements in the NHL still believed that the interlopers could somehow be defeated.

One force that could not be defeated very easily was Les Canadiens. As the Flyers faded, the bleu, blanc et rouge not only took over the league but amassed one of the most awesome records imaginable. Guy Lafleur, winner of the Art Ross and Hart Trophies, paced the Canadiens to 60 wins as against only eight losses and 12 ties. Entering the playoffs, the Flying Frenchmen — with some notable Anglophiles thrown in — didn't miss a beat. They devoured the Bruins in a four-game final earning comparisons with the very best teams of yesteryear.

To the envy of their competitors, the Habs had an inexhaustible source of talent. Brian Engblom and Bill Nyrop, who could be starters on any other defense, were added to the Mon-

afleur, Jacques Lemaire, Yvon Cournoyer and eter Mahovlich formed a potent attack. Of ourse, Bowman was a strategist without peer.

When his Canadiens collided with Philaelphia in the 1976 finals public opinion — xcept for such precincts as Pennsylvania and nvirons — was behind the Montrealers. The Iabs played classic hockey, disdained brawl-ng and epitomized the brand of game played efore goons besmirched the ice. This was the pitome of good-guy-bad-guy hockey and, hankfully, the good guys won.

Game as the Flyers were, they couldn't natch the Canadiens firepower nor oaltending. And, surprisingly, when Philaelphia tried its usual strong arm tactics, the kes of big Larry Robinson neutralized the chultzes and Kellys in nothing flat. Montreal wept the series in four games while the hockey arons breathed a collective sigh of relief.

Instead of fading into obscurity, the WHA

Above: Montreal's Larry Robinson, a player with size, strength, skill — and the necessary toughness to challenge the Flyers at their own game.

treal roster as backup backliners and Michel "Bunny" Larocque, Dryden's backup, was comparable to the best goaltenders in captivity.

One could say that the Canadiens "slumped" in 1977-78. Instead of winning 60 games, they finished with a mere 59 victories and they lost two more games than they had the previous year, tying one less. What's more, they endured a thornier trek through the playoffs and actually were defeated twice by the Bruins before socking away the Stanley Cup four games to two.

The Habs had won three championships in a row and now were on a dynastic level with the 1949 Maple Leafs, the 1958 Canadiens and the 1964 Maple Leafs, each of whom had won three straight Cups. "As long as Guy Lafleur continued to play as well as he did and Kenny Dryden and our defense, we had the goods to keep winning," said Bowman.

And win they did although cracks begai to appear in the Montreal machine wherea others clubs — the Islanders in particular – iced impressive young rosters. Michael Bossy Bryan Trottier, Denis Potvin, Clark Gillies an Bill Smith formed a competent nucleus tha drove Al Arbour's stickhandlers to the bes overall record (51-15-14) which was remark able considering that the Isles were organize in 1972, only seven years earlier.

However, questions were raised about th Islanders ability to go the route. A year earlie they were knocked out of the playoffs by rugged Toronto team and, this time, the Rang ers eliminated them in a bitter six-game set an the Broadway Blueshirts, not their cross-count rivals, made it to the finals.

For a short time, it seemed as if the Rang ers would write another Cinderella story. The beat the Habs in Game One at The Forum an

Right: "The Flower" in full stride. Guy Lafleur was one of the most exciting players of the seventies. His explosive speed, stickhandling skills and natural goal scoring ability made him a fan favorite throughout the league — and a god in Montreal.

Opposite page: Serge Savard and Ken Dryden (above) anchored the inpenetrable Montreal Defense. Scotty Bowman (below); master strategist and the winningest coach in NHL history.

ed by two goals in Game Two, also at Montreal. But Bowman's troops were not to be denied. They rallied to capture the second game and then simply took the series away from New York, winning it in five games running.

Bowman & Co. now had four straight Stanley Cups and only one other club, Toe Blake's 1956, 1957, 1958 and 1959 editions could match that mark.

Surely, the Habs had the ingredients for a fifth consecutive Cup; at least they did at season's end but a chain reaction of events, beginning with the resignation of Bowman and the retirement of Dryden would forever alter the Canadiens route and the course of hockey history in the 1980s.

CHAPTER NINE

Two Dynasties and "The Great One"

NOBODY EXPECTED THE CANADIENS' four-Cup dynasty to last forever. Injuries, trades, attrition and retirements all erode the base of every championship club as they did with Toe Blake's five-straight-Cup juggernaut of the late 1950s.

Yet there was good reason to surmise that Scott Bowman's collection of well-distributed talent would be sufficient to enable the Habs to win one more championship to bridge the decades as the 1956-60 Habs had done.

This was not to be for several reasons, starting with the abdication of Bowman behind the bench and concluding with the retirement of Ken Dryden, the goaltender magnifique, and Jacques Lemaire, one of the most creative centers of the 1970s. In between there were other compelling factors, not the least of which was the aging of premier scorer Guy Lafleur and the resultant decline of his linemates' production.

To say the least, Bowman's departure was the most traumatic since he had seemed to be a Montreal fixture for years to come. However, a front office spat with managing director Sam Pollock — Bowman expected to be named as

Pollock's successor and was stunned by the rejection — inspired Scott to leave the Canadiens to become general manager and coach of the Buffalo Sabres.

There simply was no replacing the genius of Bowman nor was there any way to find an adequate substitute for the brilliant Dryden who chose to pursue a career in law and writing. Former Canadien Bernie Geoffrion was imported as coach while the goaltending was split among Bunny Larocque, Denis Herron and Richard Sevigny.

Geoffrion's stewardship was a disaster lasting but 30 games whereupon he was replaced by Claude Ruel. The trauma notwithstanding, Montreal still managed to put healthy numbers together (47-20-13), finishing first in the Norris Division. But the absence of Bowman, Dryden, et. al. would be felt later, sealing the dynasty's end.

A changing of the guard was taking place on other fronts. When he replaced Clarence Campbell as NHL President in 1977, John Ziegler worked behind the scenes with his

World Hockey Association counterpart Howard Baldwin to end the NHL-WHA blood war and hammer out a peace pact that would satisfy both leagues.

The merger — the NHL preferred the term expansion — did not please everyone but it was the best accommodation possible. The WHA in its final season, 1978-79, iced only six teams (Edmonton, Quebec, Winnipeg, New England, Cincinnati, Birmingham and Indianapolis) but held a trump card in prodigy Wayne Gretzky who split the season between Indianpolis and Edmonton.

Although the WHA was teetering on the brink of collapse — a state of affairs it managed through its entire life — the NHL still was unsure that the rival league would, in fact, fold. After a long series of high-level conferences, a treaty was signed which enabled the WHA to gracefully expire while four of its six clubs — Oilers, Whalers, Jets and Nordiques — were welcomed to the NHL fold. Thus, hockey's bloodiest and most costly inter-league war was concluded.

To the surprise of many, some of the WHA entrants actually were competitive in the NHL despite the fact that they had been robbed of talent by their new masters. The Oilers finished fourth in the Smythe Division, qualifying for a playoff berth the first time around while Hartford did likewise in the Norris Division. Quebec and Winnipeg finished out of the running but hardly disgraced themselves.

With Dryden, Lemaire and Bowman gone from the Canadiens, the NHL's balance of power shifted slightly away from Montreal. Under coach Pat Quinn, the Philadelphia Flyers again began flexing their muscles as they had in the mid-1970s and iced a formidable squad that featured the booming shot of Reggie Leach, the indomitable spirit of Bob Clarke and solid defense fronted by Moose Dupont, Bob

Dailey and Jim Watson. The major load of goaltending was handled by young Pete Peeters who would enjoy a long NHL career.

Chasing the Flyers was an Islanders team that had disappointed in two previous playoffs but nonetheless boasted such top-liners as Michael Bossy, Bryan Trottier, Denis Potvin and Stefan Persson. "The rap against us," said Potvin, "was that we never won the big series. Losing to Toronto in 1978 and then the Rangers in 1979 didn't help our reputation."

Isles general manager Bill Torrey believed that he required one more element to produce the championship chemistry; a persistent centerman who could give hard-working Trottier some breathing room. Late in the 1979-80 season Torrey dealt Billy Harris and Dave Lewis to Los Angeles for Butch Goring and the Islanders never looked back after that.

Above: Flyers' captain Bobby Clarke wearing the evidence of his team's ill-fated flirtation with long pants.

In his new Buffalo digs, Bowman quickly developed a winner. Gil Perreault had reached the acme of a brilliant scoring career and linemate Rick Martin still pumped home winners. The Sabres finished the season with 110 points (47-17-16), second-highest in the league behind Philadelphia (48-12-20-116) and five ahead of Boston.

If there was one negative element about the 1979-80 campaign, it was the persistent problem with stability. Franchises such as Oakland, Kansas City and Cleveland failed to the embarrassment of Ziegler & Co. while the Denver franchise — alias the Colorado Rockies — continued struggling, this time with Don "Grape" Cherry coaching.

During the homestretch of the schedule, Philadelphia appeared the favorite to dethrone Montreal as Stanley Cup champion. The Flyers set a new NHL undefeated record over a 35 game period, going 25-0-10.

Before the schedule ended, all eyes turned to Lake Placid where the 1980 Winter Olympic Games were being held. As usual the Soviet Union was favored to capture the Gold Medal

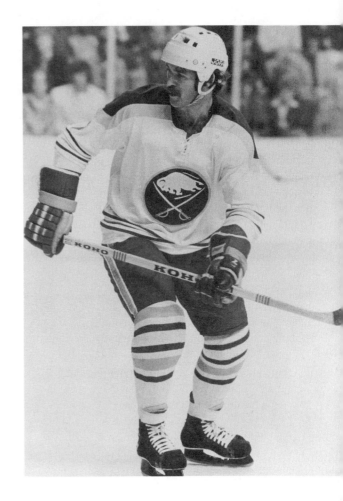

while the Americans, coached by Herb Brooks were distinct underdogs.

But as the tournament gained momentum so, too, did Uncle Sam's skaters. A game between the Americans and Russians would be pivotal particularly since some members of the U.S. team actually thought the Soviets could be beaten.

One, Eric Strobel, observed at the time, "They looked slow sometimes. We thought they were a bit too old." The Russians had struggled in previous matches against the Finns and the

Above: Buffalo's other high-scoring forward, Richard Martin, a member of the "French Connection" line with Rene Robert and Gil Perreault.

Left: Don Cherry, coach of the Boston Bruins and Colorado Rockies. His bravado proved better suited to the broadcast booth.

Canadians. The U.S. team now looked forward to meeting the Soviets and the chance to hand them their first Olympic defeat since 1968.

In the early moments of the contest, Jim Craig assisted the Yanks' lackluster defense with several outstanding saves. The Russians first drew blood, however, as Vladmir Krutov deflected a slapshot by Aleksei Kasatonov midway through the first period. The U.S. team bounced right back to tie as Buzz Schneider, on a pass from Mark Pavelich, beat the outstanding Vladislav Tretiak with a slapshot on the glove hand side of the Russian goaltender. At 17:34 Sergei Makarov scored on a pass from Vladmir Golikov, giving the Russians a 2-1 lead in the final minutes of the period. The Americans evened the score with but one second remaining on the clock, as Mark Johnson slid the rebound of a Dave Christian shot past Tretiak.

In the second period Russia regained the lead and held on to it throughout the period. The U.S. defense was weak and another Russian victory seemed imminent as the Americans struggled to even the score.

At 8:39 of the final period, the Americans knotted the score at three apiece on Mark Johnson's second goal of the game. Less than two minutes later, captain Mike Eruzione scored the go-ahead goal for the Americans and gave them their first advantage of the contest.

With ten minutes remaining in the game, the Russians tried to wear out the Americans with line changes every forty-five seconds. Brooks responded, telling his charges, "Play your game. Play your game." Whenever the Americans would play defensively Brooks would pull them from the ice and put on another line. This strategy worked, and it was the

Russians, not the Americans, who were on the ropes now, as the Russians lost their composure and began dumping the puck in.

At the final buzzer the score read U.S.-4, USSR -3. The Russians had been defeated, and the underdog American squad became the Cinderella team of the century.

In their final game, the U.S. team faced a tough Finnish squad and needed a win for the gold medal. In the first period of the game Jukka Porvari scored, giving Finland a 1-0 lead — the sixth time in seven games that America trailed and had to come from behind to win. The United States evened it on Steve Christoff's backhander, then gave the lead back to the Finns, as Mikko Leinonen (who would one day play for Herb Brooks as a New York Ranger) potted a power-play tally. At the end of two periods, the Americans were down, 2-1.

Right: Ken Morrow, one of the hero's of the U.S. Olympic team's 1980 gold medal, jumped to the NHL after the Games to play with the New York Islanders.

Right: A whale of a family! The NHL's first father and sons act teamed Gordie Howe (center) with sons Mark (left) and Marty (right) for the Hartford Whalers.

Two and a half minutes into the third period, Dave Christian split the Finnish defense and passed to Phil Verchota who powered a drive past the Finnish goaltender. Less than four minutes later Rob McClanahan scored the go-ahead goal giving the Americans a 3-2 lead. For the remainder of the game Jim Craig's goaltending held the Finns scoreless, and America rallied once more to make the final score, 4-2. America had won its second gold medal in hockey, dethroning the Soviets who had not lost a championship since 1960, the year Herb Brooks had been the last player cut from the U.S. Olympic squad.

The American victory was only one of several upheavals on ice. As the NHL entered the 1980s the professional game took on a new face. The success of teenager Wayne Gretzky inspired teams to sign younger players, and

the youngsters in turn put the accent on offense instead of defense — with astonishing results.

During the 1980-81 season the league's twenty-one clubs averaged 7.7 goals, the highest since the NHL had introduced the center red line in 1943. Even first-rate goalies such as Tony Esposito of the Chicago Blackhawks were victimized. A year later the average climbed again, this time to a staggering 8.03. "It used to be you'd get three or four goals and you were a cinch to win it," said the late Penguins' general manager Baz Bastien. "Now you can score five, and there's a good chance you'll lose."

Typical of the trend were the scores on one night: Boston 10, Quebec 1; Toronto 9, Los Angeles 4; Pittsburgh 7, Philadelphia 2. "Today," said Blackhawk goalie Tony Esposito, "you go through a whole season without a shutout."

The trend continued through the 1982-83

campaign. On one night in which five games were played, 55 goals were scored. One hundred and ten goals in two nights!

There were several explanations for the new trend. Increased use of the slapshot had enabled even average players to propel the puck at speeds of up to 100 miles per hour, faster than ever. Teams employed back-up (less competent) goaltenders more often than at any time in the past. Many teams have theorized that high-scoring hockey, by its very nature, is more appealing. "Fans like to see 6-5 games more than 1-0 games," said Wayne Gretzky. "I know we prefer them, too."

Others have suggested that the art of defense, quite simply, has been lost on the younger players. "No one knows how to play defense when it's three-on-three in your own end," said scout Claude Ruel of the Montreal Canadiens. "That's why so many loose pucks are scored — because somebody isn't covering his area, and the puck comes out to some guy who's all alone. You can't let people stand around alone in the middle."

Some experts predicted that the trend toward inflationary scoring would be halted by the mid-1980s and that there would be a return to more defensive-oriented, lower scoring games. "The trend has been to eliminate the older, experienced players and get the younger, quicker, offensively aggressive players, and, as a result, the scores went up," said Glen Sather, general manager of the Edmonton Oilers. "The younger players were so good offensively that, after a few years, the area in which they'll improve is defense."

Soon after the Olympic games had been concluded, a number of Uncle Sam's skaters signed with NHL teams. In 1981 former Olympic coach Herb Brooks signed a contract with the New York Rangers. A year later Bob Johnson, a successful coach at the University of Wisconsin, was signed by the Calgary Flames of the NHL. It marked the first time that a Canadian major league club had signed an American collegiate coach.

Even more significantly, in terms of the major strides being taken by American players, was the fact that the Washington Capitals signed eighteen-year-old Bobby Carpenter of Peabody, Massachusetts, to an NHL contract in 1981. Carpenter became the first American to leap from high school to the NHL, yet veterans such as Bobby Clarke still proved valuable. This sequence of events had great meaning to serious hockey critics who chart the winds of change in the sport. It signified a major upheaval in the

Above: When the Washington Capitals drafted Bobby Carpenter as their first pick in 1981, Sports Illustrated labeled him the "can't miss kid." Carpenter became the first American-born player to score 50 goals.

one of the main reasons why we won four straight Stanley Cups."

The advent of the Islanders dynasty was not altogether unexpected. With Bill Smith and Glenn (Chico) Resch in goal, the Isles had the foundation of a big winner considering the maturation of super-defenseman Denis Potvin and the accumulation of such top forwards as Bossy, Gillies and Trottier. When Butch Goring was obtained in March 1980, g.m. Bill Torrey's handpicked club was ready to make its move.

Unlike previous seasons when the Islanders were outhit (Maple Leafs, 1978) or outhustled (Rangers, 1979), coach Al Arbour got his club to percolate as never before. "Butch (Goring) gave us that center ice balance we never had before," said Arbour.

As a result the Isles steamed to the 1980 Stanley Cup finals where they defeated the

Dynamic Duo!
The Islanders' goaltending team of Billy Smith (above) and Glenn "Chico" Resch (right) was the foundation on which the team's 4-Cup dynasty was built.

balance of power, on a par with the steady rise in the number of Europeans playing in North America. Americans were making their biggest inroads into the NHL.

Toronto Star hockey analyst Rex MacLeod frankly conceded that Americans might dominate the sport by 1990. "Like it or not," said MacLeod, "there is evidence that Americans will be in the majority in the NHL in a few years."

Some of the best evidence was produced by the 1980 Olympians. Defenseman Ken Morrow moved directly from Lake Placid to Uniondale, New York, where he became an instant regular on the New York Islanders. "Kenny," said Islanders coach Al Arbour, "was

Flyers in six games. The final game, played on May 24, 1980, said it all for the Islanders' perseverance. They blew a two-goal lead in the third period and appeared ready to capitulate when Smith rescued them with a couple of spectacular saves forcing the game into overtime. Appropriately, at 7:11 of the first sudden-death period, Bob Nystrom took a pass from John Tonelli and one-timed the puck past goalie Pete Peeters. The first leg of the Islanders' dynasty was in place.

A year later the Nassau skaters topped the NHL with 110 points (48-18-14) and then charged past Toronto, Edmonton, the Rangers and Minnesota for their second straight championship. "We felt we could play hockey any way the other team wanted to play," said Potvin, "and beat them."

The record underlined his point. In 1981-82 the Isles again topped the league (54-16-10) with 118 points. They opened the playoffs against an inferior Pittsburgh team which suddenly got hot in the best-of-five series, extending New York to a fifth game. Trailing by two goals in the third, the Islanders staged a late rally and won in overtime.

That done they beat the Rangers in a six-game set and then swept Quebec and Vancouver four games each, thus becoming the first American team ever to win three consecutive Stanley Cups.

By 1982-83, Wayne Gretzky and the Edmonton Oilers had become a force in the NHL. Backed by such luminaries as Paul Coffey, Mark Messier, Kevin Lowe, Jari Kurri and Grant Fuhr, Gretzky paced the former WHA club to new heights including first place in the Smythe Division.

For the first time, Edmonton emerged as a

Above: Mike Bossy, known as "Mr. 50" for his goal-scoring consistency. Right: Denis Potvin, the Islanders' gritty captain.

Stanley Cup threat. The Oilers demolished Winnipeg, Calgary and Chicago in the first three rounds while the Islanders trimmed Washington, the Rangers and Boston to go head-to-head with the Oilers.

For all intents and purposes, the finals were settled in Game One at Edmonton where the Oilers strafed Bill Smith from every conceivable angle and came away with not a single goal. Duane Sutter's first period score was all the Islanders needed although they got insurance from Ken Morrow with 12 seconds remaining.

New York then swept the next three games and had an unprecedented — for an American team — four consecutive Stanley Cups and immediately prepared their "Drive For Five."

Under ordinary circumstances, the Islanders might well have equalled the record established by the Canadiens, circa 1956-60. The Isles and Oilers again met in the finals only this time the series opened at Nassau Coliseum and the scenario also was reversed. An early Edmonton goal was all Grant Fuhr needed and the Oilers escaped with a win in the first game. The Islanders pounced back with a vengeance in Game Two but then the series took a curious turn. Instead of the next two games scheduled for Edmonton, the NHL decided to have the next three straight slated for Northlands Coliseum.

The combination of playing three games in a row on hostile ice not to mention an unconscionable spate of injuries was just too much for the Islanders to overcome. They lost all three games at Edmonton and thereby relinquished the Stanley Cup.

Considering the Oilers mix of collective youth and talent, they had all the ingredients for a long Stanley Cup reign while age had

Right: Guess why this publicity montage became a collector's item? It was sent out by the Oilers publicity office — and guess who's name is spelled incorrectly?

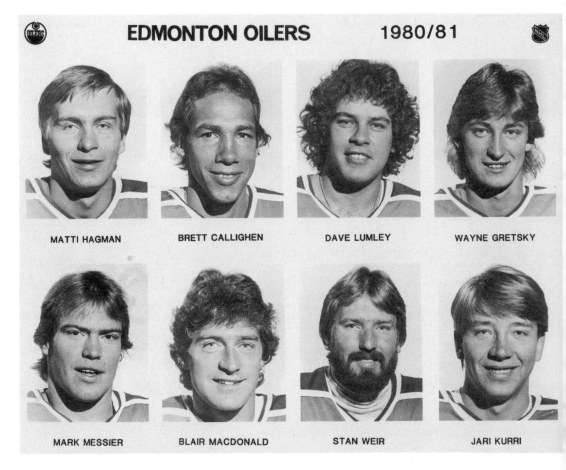

EDMONTON OILERS   1980/81

MATTI HAGMAN   BRETT CALLIGHEN   DAVE LUMLEY   WAYNE GRETSKY

MARK MESSIER   BLAIR MACDONALD   STAN WEIR   JARI KURRI

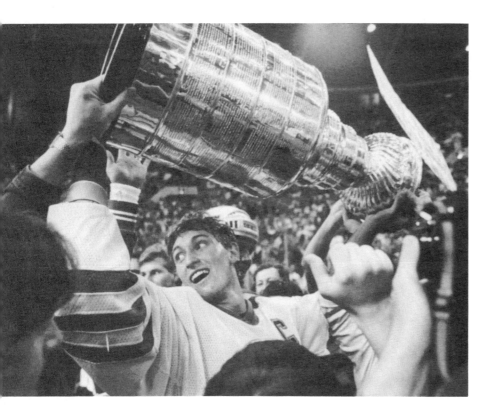

The Firewagon Dynasty!
The Edmonton Oilers of the 1980s won the Stanley Cup 5 times in 7 seasons by playing a freewheeling, fast-paced style of hockey.
Left: Captain Wayne Gretzky raises the Cup. "The Great One," as he is called won the Hart Trophy (most valuable player in the NHL) 9 times in ten seasons.
Below: Mark Messier played a physical brand of hockey with intensity and skill.

permanently braked the Islanders. Edmonton won another championship in 1985. "We don't want to go down in history as one of the great teams who ended up winning only two Stanley Cups in a row," said Coffey.

However, it wasn't to be. Like the mighty Red Wings, who failed to win three in a row during the 1950s; like the fast-living Blackhawks of the 1960s and the Bruins of the 1970s, the Oilers suffered from a fatal flaw; they lacked the dedication — call it seriousness — of the true dynasty and, inevitably, they were a victim of their shortcomings.

During the 1986 playoffs, when they appeared to be on the lip of a third straight Stanley Cup, they lost to the inferior (on paper) Calgary Flames in as ignominious a manner as possible. (A clearing pass from behind the Edmonton net delivered by defenseman Steve Smith caromed off goalie Grant Fuhr's leg and into the Oilers goal and they never recovered.) With Edmonton disposed of, the Canadiens skated to the finals and defeated Calgary for Mon-

treal's last moment of Stanley Cup glory.

The loss to Calgary did not diminish the value of Edmonton's stars. Gretzky had become the king of hockey and his reign was

Above: Gretzky terrorizes opponents with precision passing and one of the most unpredictable shots in hockey.

supreme, except, perhaps for the arrival of a large French-Canadian named Mario Lemieux.

Mario won the Clader Trophy as rookie-of-the-year in 1985, based on some very impressive (43 goals, 57 assists, for 100 points - 10 behind Gretzky's rookie (in the WHA) stats. But the Penguins died relatively early in the campaign and Mario was variously described as a "floater" (by Don Cherry), a "prima donna" (by some teammates), and one who failed to lift Pittsburgh in the homestretch when the Penguins ignominiously lost all semblance of a playoff bound team. "He had a lot of skills even

then," says Cherry, "but there were parts of his game — his intensity, for one thing — that left a lot to be desired."

Nonetheless, even in his rookie year Lemieux was doing very Gretzky-like things, such as creating stars out of unknowns. Warren Young was exhibit A. "Do you want to know how good Mario was in his rookie year?" asked St. Louis special scout Bob Plager. "In 1984-85 a 29-year old guy (Young) who couldn't make the NHL came out to their camp. They put him with Lemieux, and he scored 40 goals. He became a free agent the next year, signs with Detroit for a million dollars, and does almost nothing."

To put Lemieux's contribution as a

armaker into perspective, one only has to com-are Warren Young's 1984-85 Pittsburgh stats ith his 1985-86 Red Wings numbers. As a enguin skating alongside Lemieux, Young roduced 40 goals and 32 assists for 72 points. he following year, by contrast, he totalled only 2 goals and 24 assists for 46 points. That meant drop of 18 goals and 8 assists for 26 points. It so meant that the Penguins coach Bob Berry ad to find a replacement for Young in 1985-86.

In 1985-86, Berry put the veteran Terry uskowski on Lemieux's line and the gears eatly meshed through mid-season. The Pen-

guins had become playoff contenders and Mario had grown from a first-rate rookie to a FORCE. "After Gretzky," said then Red Wings coach Jacques Demers, "Mario has become the sec-ond-best hockey player in the NHL.

"In his second year," said Berry, "he was not only a year older, but he showed it. He became a great two-way player and he's only going to get better." So much for "Mario the Floater!"

By mid-season (1985-86) the Penguins were in a dogfight with the New York Rangers, New York Islanders and New Jersey Devils for a

Left: Mario Lemieux, pos-sessing the skill of Gretzky with the size of Messier.

people who understand hockey understand tha Mario is under 20 and he will be up there, too He's so big. He's so strong. And he has thos long, long moves."

in any comparison between the two, siz must immediately be considered. Lemieux (6 4, 215 pounds) has the look of a dreadnough or, if you fancy pre-historic monsters, the de scription offered by Boston Bruins defensema Mike Milbury. "Lemieux,' said Milbury, "is lik a pterodactyl — one of those flying reptile He's big, has a long reach, skates like hell, an is real strong."

At 6-0, 170 pounds (if he's lucky) Gretzk appeared almost fragile, yet opponents agre that his anticipation, his total view of the ic has enabled him to avoid potentially damagin bodychecks. An important distinction whic had helped keep Gretzky ahead of Lemieu had been the presence of superior offensiv defenseman Paul Coffey, who helped to embe

playoff berth. Lemieux was carrying the Penguins. Soon, the Devils — Jersey's Lemieux equivalent was Kirk Muller — faded out of sight. Mario kept scoring

Then it happened! The unthinkable was spoken. In January 1986 Randy Cunneyworth, a Pittsbuurgh left winger, said, "There's no question in my mind that Mario's the best player in the National Hockey League and probably the world."

For the first time, Lemieux was being placed on Gretzky's plateau, if not higher. Was this simply Penguins hype? Not necessarily. Willy Lindstrom, one of Gretzky's close friends — and a former teammate — played on a line in Edmonton with Gretzky and then with Lemieux in Pittsburgh. Lindstrom, more than anyone, is capable of a fair, first hand evaluation.

"Certainly," said Lindstrom, "they are the two most talented players in the league, but the

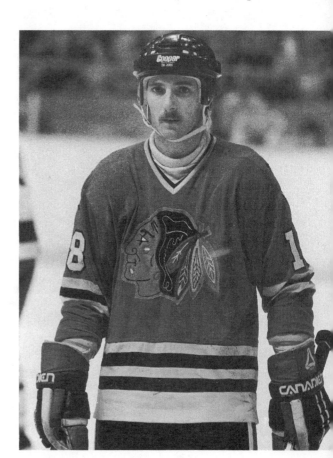

sh his point total when he was with the Oilers.

Gretzky, Messier, et. al. got their acts together in 1987 and again in 1988 when the Oilers again won successive Stanley Cups. But during the summer of 1988 Oilers owner Peter Pocklington detonated what has been described as the greatest trade in hockey history.

Gretzky was dealt to the Los Angeles Kings – recently acquired by entrepreneur Bruce McNall — along with Mike Krushelnyski and Marty McSorley. In return, Edmonton obtained Jimmy Carson, Martin Gelinas, the Kings first round draft choices in 1989, 1991 and 1993 entry drafts and an estimated $20 million cash.

Reverberations from *the trade* shook Edmonton through the season and would have long-range effects on the Oilers. The Kings swiftly benefitted from McNall's move. Gretzky became an instant hero in Tinseltown and crowds began filling The Great Western Forum in Inglewood in larger numbers than ever before. Even better, from an artistic viewpoint,

Four Stars of the 1980s: Clockwise from the top far left: Peter Stastny of the Quenbec Nordiques, Ray Bourque of Boston, Lanny McDonald of Calgary and Denis Savard of Chicago.

the Kings leapfrogged over the Oilers, finishing second in the Smythe Division behind the Flames.

Adding insult to injury, Los Angeles disposed of Edmonton four games to three in a gripping series that added even more lustre to Gretzky's image. The arduous battle drained the Kings who were then swept by Calgary in four games. The Flames, coached by Terry Crisp, vanquished the Blackhawks in five games and, finally, the Canadiens in six to win their first Stanley Cup.

Interestingly, the Flames leading scorer over the entire season was New York City-born Joe Mullen, who finished seventh on the list. The leader for the second year in a row was not Gretzky but rather the new king of hockey, Mario Lemieux.

"Le Magnifique" reached the scoring pinnacle as the NHL prepared for a revolutionary new era that would be pockmarked with controversy — including big-league hockey's first major strike — big bucks and expansion that oldtimers never would have dreamed possible.

CHAPTER TEN
The Tumultuous Nineties

SPORTS ILLUSTRATED MAGAZINE IS NOT INCLINED to feature hockey on its cover during the off-season but it made an exception after some startling events in the summer of 1989.

For the first time in NHL history a flock of stars from the Soviet Union were imported to North America where they would grace the rosters of big-league teams.

The *SI* cover depicted defensemen Viacheslav Fetisov and Sergei Starikov standing amid tall weeds in the New Jersey Meadowlands with the Byrne Arena, home of the Devils, looming in the background. Fetisov, captain of legendary Russian Olympic and World Championship teams, was signed by Devils owner Dr. John McMullen along with second-stringer Starikov.

Meanwhile, the Vancouver Canucks nabbed Vladimir "Tank" Krutov and Igor Larionov, who were expected to ignite the malingering franchise. Sergei Makarov, who had been the balance wheel of the Krutov-Larionov line in Russia, was separated from his pals and inked by the Calgary Flames.

All of these were older players, considered expendable by the higher Soviet hockey authorities although none of the Russians — especially national coach Viktor Tikhonov — were pleased to see their players uprooted from the leagues of Mother Russia.

And they were singularly furious when the Buffalo Sabres, over their strenuous objections, lured young Alexander Mogilny to the United States and refused any suggestions that he be returned. Clearly, the Russian Revolution in the NHL had begun with both a bang and a whimper.

Some of the players — Makarov in particular — riveted the attention of NHL fans who were unaccustomed to the effortless skating, radar passes and overall knowledge of hockey exuded by the Soviets. Others were less successful. Starikov wound up in the minors while the eternally overweight Krutov was virtually booed out of British Columbia.

Fetisov played commendably if not up to his former world class form. In mid-season the Devils added Fetisov's former partner, Alexe

decided the issue for the Kings. Calgary never recovered from the rapid explosion and the Flames would undergo a wrenching period of torment before they would again right themselves in 1992-93.

Everyone had expected a magical Gretzky-Lemieux scoring race but nobody had accounted for the excruciating back problems which would afflict Mario from the homestretch of the season — he missed 21 of the Penguins final 22 games — to the present. The Great One was not without his own aches but Wayne missed only seven games and annexed the scoring title on the strength of 40 goals and 142 points.

In terms of pure goal-scoring ability Calgary castoff Brett Hull burst on the scene with all the glitz that his father, Bobby "The Golden Jet" Hull, had exhibited in the 1960s. Brett blitzed goaltenders to the tune of 72 red

Kasatonov, who ironically, had become estranged from his buddy because of political differences with Slava. Nevertheless, the two defenseman forgot politics once on the ice and formed an effective blue line tandem for the Devils, who finished second in the Patrick Division (two points behind the Rangers) for the first time in franchise history.

During the regular season Calgary looked good enough to repeat as Stanley Cup champions. The Flames finished with the second best points mark (behind Boston) with basically the same squad as the previous year. But coach Terry Crisp and his skaters ran into a white hot Los Angeles sextet in Round One. Overtime winners by Tony Granato in Game Three and Mike Krushelnyski in the decisive sixth game

Alexander Mogilny, (above) the Buffalo Sabres talented offensive threat, and (right) Vancouver's Pavel Bure — two of the success stories of the much-hyped "red invasion." Both players were acquired by NHL franchises early in their careers.

la creme of the NHL and for that much deb was paid to defenseman Raymond Bourqu who took the Norris Trophy and also was factor in Boston's parade to the Stanley Cu finals.

Unquestionably the most emphatic sui prise was generated by Edmonton. Seeming shredded by the loss of such Cup-winners a Gretzky and Paul Coffey, the Oilers were no regarded as contenders until they finished sec ond in the Smythe Division with an impressiv 90 points, nine behind league-leading Calgary

But Gretzky's departure thrust Mar Messier to the fore. Having played second fid dle to The Great One since 1979, Messier too over the captaincy and instantly became th leader and guiding force of the Oilers. Nick named "Moose," Messier virtually willed Ed monton to a dominating position. He scored 4 goals, 84 assists and 129 points, which was th best ever for him, and sufficient for the Har Trophy.

lights and guided the Blues to a four-games-to-one playoff victory over Toronto. A non-belligerent like his father, Hull also won the Lady Byng Trophy.

Under Harry Sinden's leadership, the Bruins once again remained among la creme de

Above: "The Golden Brett" — Brett Hull, the most potent scorer in St. Louis history and one of the most gifted natural goal scorers since his father Bobby, "The Golden Jet", terrorized the NHL in the 1960s.

Right: Over the years the Boston Bruins have suffered more injuries to key players than any other club. In the case of Cam Neely (right), a freak leg injury sidelined the rugged 50-goal scorer for most of two seasons. At his healthy best Neely plays a hard-hitting brand of hockey that reminds many observers of Gordie Howe in his prime.

Left: After a long and successful career with the 5-time Stanley Cup champion Edmonton Oilers, Mark Messier moved to New York in 1990-91, where he became the Rangers' captain. Messier responded by leading the Broadway Blueshirts to a first place regular season finish and won his second Hart trophy as league MVP.

When Los Angeles knocked off defending champion Calgary in the first playoff round, it suddenly opened the games for Edmonton. The Oilers required a tough seven games before beating Winnipeg, routed Los Angeles in four and then took Chicago in six although at one point the Blackhawks led the series two games to one. However, Messier got hot and the Oilers entered the finals against the Bruins who had been regarded as a worthy opponent.

Boston did register one win but that was all; the Oilers had the required four faster than most thought and an amazing fifth Stanley Cup for veterans such as Messier and Kevin Lowe. Perhaps the most arresting fact of all was that the triumph came without first-string goalie Grant Fuhr between the pipes. Sidelined because of a bum shoulder, Fuhr was replaced by young Bill Ranford who produced a 24-16-9 record during the regular season and excelled during the playoffs as well.

One conclusion produced by the 1989-90

season was that the Soviet players, if properly selected, could be major assets to NHL teams. Makarov won the Calder Trophy as rookie-of-the-year while Fetisov and Kasatonov helped New Jersey make the playoffs. Larionov won the hearts of Vancouver fans and the chase was on to exploit the mother lode of talent in Mother Russia.

The Detroit Red Wings captured a prize in Central Red Army star Sergei Fedorov who bade good-bye to the Central Red Army team and, without permission, skedaddled to the Motor City where he became almost as popular as captain Steve Yzerman.

Ever since the successful debut of Peter Stastny, a Slovak, in the early 1980s, NHL scouts also kept an Argus eye on Czechoslovakia. Prospects such as Bobby Holik (Hartford), Petr Nedved (Vancouver) and Zdeno Ciger (New

Jersey) stepped right onto the varsity roster and were able to compete on favorable terms with the big-leaguers.

The new decade spelled growth on other levels. After much soul-searching, league owners decided to expand to San Jose, California in 1991-92 and then would add two more teams — Ottawa and Tampa Bay — the following season. Placing an NHL club in Florida was considered a huge risk by many but it was felt that the league had to keep pace with the ever expanding NBA if it was to remain a big money maker.

What added optimism to the Florida move was a crowd of 25,581 that jammed St. Petersburg's Suncoast Dome. Although it was only an NHL exhibition game, the audience was the largest recorded for professional match in North America.

Left: Ed "The Eagle" Belfour of the Blackhawks walked away with the Calder Trophy (rookie of the year) and the Vezina (best goatender) in 1991.
Above: Detroit's captain Steve Yzerman — always an offensive threat.

pressed, especially Sweden's Mats Sundin of Quebec and Jaromir Jagr, the long-haired Czech who became a teammate of Mario Lemieux in Pittsburgh.

Although the Oilers finished with a modest .500 record (37-37-6), nobody was counting out Edmonton once the playoffs began; and for good reason. The Oilers caught fire in the very first round, beating Calgary in a full seven-game series and then upset the Kings in six games to reach the Conference Championships.

In the Wales Conference all eyes were on the Penguins. Despite all of Mario Lemieux's

The 1990-91 regular season proved to be a onanza for Gretzky and the Kings. They finshed atop the Smythe Division (46-24-10-102) or the third best overall record in the league nd the Great One again topped all scorers vith 163 points (41-122-163), 32 points ahead of unner-up Brett Hull.

Detroit's addition of Federov proved wise. Ie was the leading rookie scorer overall with 9 points and topped all freshmen on the basis f 31 goals. Other foreign rookies also im-

bove: Chris Chelios, an American-born defenseman nd two time Norris Trophy-winner, was dealt by the 1ontreal Canadiens to the Chicago Blackhawks for orward Denis Savard — arguably one of the worst ades in Habs history.

ight: Theoren Fleury, one of only five Calgary players o reach the 100 point mark in a season — and one of he smallest players in pro hockey.

abundant talents, he had not been able to spearhead Pittsburgh to a championship and now that he had reached his prime, critics wondered whether he would ever achieve that goal.

Doubts were even deeper when the New Jersey Devils moved to a three- games-to-two lead in the opening Patrick Division round. Like a true champion, Lemieux rallied his club to victories in Games Six and Seven, eliminating the Devils. Pittsburgh then routed the Washington Capitals in five games and took Boston in six although the Bruins had won the first pair of the Wales Conference finals.

Above: For years the Vancouver Canuks searched for a dynamic performer who would lead them to the upper echelon. They finally found him in Trevor Linden, a Western Canadian who came into his own in the early 1990s. Linden's natural leadership inspired President Pat Quinn to name him team captain.

When the upstart Minnesota North Star bumped Edmonton out of contention in a five game Campbell Conference finals, the unlikel prospect of Pittsburgh playing Minnesota fo The Stanley Cup became reality.

To the astonishment of everyone, the Nortl Stars beat Pittsburgh in the Civic Arena opene The Penguins won Game Two but again Min nesota showed its stuff by taking a two-games to-one series lead. Try as they might, the Star couldn't get it all together in Game Four i which the Penguins prevailed 5-3. The Pen guins then wrapped up the series, 6-4 and 8- to bring Lord Stanley's silverware to The Stee City for the first time.

Of particular significance was the man be hind the Penguins bench — Bob Johnson. Alia "The Badger," Johnson again demonstrated tha ex-collegiate coaches had the right stuff for win ning in the pro ranks. Little did anyone realiz that tragedy would strike before the next sea son had begun. Johnson was afflicted with brain tumour and died before the first pucl was dropped in the 1991-92 season.

The Penguins decided that Scott Bowmai would be the most appropriate choice to re place Johnson. Although Bowman had lon; ago forsaken coaching for a front office posi tion, he accepted general manager Crai; Patrick's offer and proved that, given time, h could stir a winning potion.

For most of the season, Pittsburgh seemec to be suffering from the fallout of Johnson' death and there was concern in the Penguin dressing room that a second Stanley Cup wa not going to be possible.

Competition in the Patrick Division wa keen. Under coach Roger Neilson, the Ranger remained in first place for most of the seasor and were actually considered a favorite to wir their first Stanley Cup since 1940.

Then it happened. After long and ofter

Left: There were serious doubts whether this super-star would even make it into the 1990s, due to a chronic back injury which required surgery. Mario Lemieux not only came back, he led the Penguins to two successive Stanley Cup victories (1991, 1992), capturing the Conn Smythe trophy as playoff MVP on both occasions.

harsh negotiations between National Hockey League Players' Association executive director Bob Goodenow and league owners, the players called a walkout. The unprecedented strike shook the hockey world like no other event in memory. Instantly, the schedule ground to a halt while NHL President John Ziegler and Goodenow attempted to forge an agreement.

But the newly-militant players were not about to concede anything. They believed that they had been mistreated by management over the years and now wanted to extract the best deal possible. They backed Goodenow to the hilt and appeared quite willing to sacrifice the entire season to win their points.

Just when it seemed that all hope for resurrecting the season was lost, the two sides struck a deal and the games resumed with varying effects on different teams. "The strike hurt us," charged Roger Neilson. "We were in a groove and playoff-ready when they walked out and we lost that edge by the time we got back."

The Rangers did finish with the best overall record but they were not the same once the playoffs began. They just barely ousted the Devils in a bitter seven-game series whereupon they then collided with the Penguins. When in the second game, Mario Lemieux was struck down by a vicious slash delivered by Adam Graves, all signs suggested that the Rangers would oust Pittsburgh. But the Penguins rallied behind Ron Francis splendid backup centering and Tom Barrasso's clutch goaltending to push the Rangers out of the playoffs.

Lemieux, who had suffered a broken hand,

returned for the Boston-Pittsburgh series and proved his mettle as both a leader and scorer. The Bruins were then eliminated, setting the stage for a Stanley Cup final between Pittsburgh and Chicago.

In the opening game at Pittsburgh Civic Arena, the Blackhawks checked well and jumped into a three-goal lead. Goalie Ed Belfour, one of the league's best, had the goods to nurse the margin to victory. Or did he?

With the speed and force of a hurricane the Penguins forced the Blackhawks to take cover and, thanks to some extraordinary stickhandling and scoring by Jaromir Jagr, Pittsburgh rallied for a win.

Mike Keenan's Blackhawks never recovered from the shock. Lemieux & Co. swept the next three games to become two-time winners. And nobody ever again accused Lemieux of failing to be a championship player.

CHAPTER ELEVEN

1992-93
Totally Bizarre

IF ONE WERE TO SUMMARIZE in one word the NHL avalcade of events from the summer of 1992 through June 1993 the term would have to be "strange."

Bizarre wouldn't be an inappropriate label either when one considers the Eric Lindros Career of June 1992 when first the Philadelphia Flyers believed that they had dealt for The Next One only to learn minutes before the annual Entry Draft in Montreal that Quebec Nordiques resident Marcel Aubut also had cut a deal with the New York Rangers.

L'Affaire Lindros proved yet another embarrassment to the outgoing John Ziegler administration and a headache to interim president Gil Stein, who previously had been the league's chief counsel. To settle the Lindros tug-of-war, the league appointed a special arbitrator, Larry Bertuzzi, who then went about the business of grilling everyone connected with the deals.

For a time the Rangers believed they had the edge in a transaction that would have sent goalie John Vanbiesbrouck, defenseman James Patrick, forwards Darren Turcotte and Tony Amonte as well as an estimated $15 million cash to Les Nordiques. But Bertuzzi ruled that the Flyers, who had made the offer before New York intruded, was legally entitled to Lindros. In exchange, Quebec obtained goalie Ron Hextall, defensemen Steve Duchesne and Kerry Huffman, forward Mike Ricci and the rights to Swedish sniper Peter Forsberg as well as a similar cash windfall.

Having wiped mud off the NHL's face by finally concluding the Lindros settlement, interim president Stein then went about the business of improving the league image. Unlike his predecessor, he fervently courted the media and spent much of July, August and September 1992 criss-crossing the continent, holding press conferences in almost every NHL city while, in the minds of cynical newsmen, campaigning for the upcoming league commissionership.

With Ziegler well-ensconced in the wings, the NHL had decided that it would take a more progressive approach. Los Angeles Kings owner Bruce McNall — considered a liberal among

Right: Czech Jaromir Jagr broke into the NHL with the Pittsburgh Penguins in 1990-91, and played a key role in Pittsburgh's two league championships. Jagr, who turned 20 in his sophomore year played an even greater role with the Penguins in 1992-93 with captain Mario Lemieux sidelined due to illness. He has proven to be one of the league's budding stars who should carry hockey through the next decade.

his colleagues — replaced conservative William Wirtz, owner of the Chicago Blackhawks, as chairman of the Board of Governors. McNall, who had studied the highly-successful National Basketball Association, believed that hockey people had much to learn from their hoop rivals. McNall pushed for creation of a commissioner in the NBA manner and launched an intensive search for a new leader.

Stein remained a top candidate for the job and campaigned vigorously through the autumn of 1992 but he had two strikes against him — his age and his much-criticized decision to forgo game suspensions for severely penalized players. McNall and his fellow owners decided that a vibrant, young leader was needed although Stein, well into the 60s, certainly was full of vim, vigor and vitality. But when Stein ruled that players should serve their suspensions on off-days and be permitted to play de-

spite the suspensions, it inspired ridicule from coast-to-coast.

However, the interim president earned kudos for enforcing the league's new anti-goon legislation. Increased use of the "instigator" penalty resulted in a noticeable decrease in fighting. Also, in the early weeks of the 1992-93 season officials were cracking down on restraining fouls such as stick-holding with more energy than anyone can remember. While this helped open up the ice to a certain extent, there also were complaints of too many whistles and later in the season the referees reverted to their laissez-faire attitude of previous years.

When the season opened, Pittsburgh was given a decent chance to win a third-straight Stanley Cup but the Rangers, who had finished with the best overall record, also received considerable support because of their starry lineup.

Then, the season started and strange things

appened. Although the Rangers added even
more high-priced talent to an already wealthy
group of athletes, the Broadway Blueshirts
ardly sprinted from the post. A major source
f trouble was a festering rift between captain
Mark Messier and coach Roger Neilson. Ever
ince the Rangers were eliminated from the
992 playoffs, Messier not-so-subtly cam-
aigned against his coach, suggesting that
Neilson advocated too conservative a style of
lay that cramped the club's offensive talents.

Attempts at reconciling the captain and
he coach extended through the early months
f the season but failed. Meanwhile, two blocs
merged on the team; the anti-Messier-pro-
Neilson group and another clique comprised
f former Edmonton Oilers led by Messier,
Adam Graves and Jeff Beukeboom. Eventually,
Messier prevailed. Neilson was fired in mid-
eason and replaced by Ron Smith, who had
een coaching the Rangers American League
arm club in Binghamton.

Meanwhile, the Penguins fulfilled their
otices and moved to the top of the competitive
Patrick Division. Mario Lemieux never looked
etter, scoring almost at will and well-supported
y Ron Francis, Jaromir Jagr, Rick Tocchet, Joe
Mullen and Kevin Stevens. Tom Barrasso gave
Pittsburgh world-class goaltending and Scott
Bowman's coaching looked as good as it ever
id in his halcyon days with the Montreal
Canadiens.

The rest of the Patrick Division featured a
ascinating dogfight between the Islanders,
Devils, Flyers and Capitals. Lindros instantly
aptured the imagination of Spectrum fans with
 spectacular opening night, game-winning goal
gainst New Jersey and looked every bit as
aluable as his multi-million dollar price tag.

But a chain reaction of problems, includ-
ng off-ice difficulties as well as a spate of inju-
ies, braked Lindros' progress and severely

damaged Philadelphia's bid for a playoff berth.

The Capitals early start was slowed by a
bad trade in which crack scorer Dino Ciccarelli
had been sent to Detroit for Kevin Miller who
briefly teamed up with older brother, Kelly, at
Capital Centre. Kevin was lost in Washington
and eventually was dispatched to St.Louis. In
time coach Terry Murray straightened out his
lineup and the Caps became playoff contenders. Although their offense lacked a super-
scorer, they obtained considerable support from

*Above: After toiling in underrated obscu-
rity through the late 1980s in Long
Island, center Pat Lafontaine was traded
to Buffalo where he bloomed as one of the
league's best offensive players.*

a high-scoring defense led by Al Iafrate, Kevin Hatcher and Sylvain Cote.

The Islanders, who played most of their first-half season games on the road, had hoped to reach the New Year at or near the .500 mark. "If we can do that," said general manager Don Maloney, "we can make the playoffs." The Isles did achieve their objective but floundered in mid-January until goalie Mark Fitzpatrick helped defeat the Devils at Byrne Arena, thereby putting Al Arbour's skaters on track for a post-season berth.

Under new coach Herb Brooks, the Devils appeared to be short at center until the taciturn Russian, Alexander Semak, emerged as one of the best-kept secrets in the league. Brooks continued tinkering with his lineup through the half-way mark while keeping his club in the middle of the pack. In time the Semak-Valeri Zelepukin-Claude Lemieux line surfaced as one of the Patrick's Division's most formidable trios

By mid-season the league had narrowed down its choices for commissioner to two candidates, Gil Stein and a hitherto unknown, Gary Bettman who previously had been third in command at the National Basketball Association. Because of Stein's long-time NHL connection it was freely assumed that he was the favorite to get the post but the interim president had angered some power brokers with his unabashed campaign for the commissionership while others favored a completely fresh face on the scene.

The appointment of Bettman was an NHL milestone because he was so different from his predecessors, John Ziegler, Clarence Campbell

Right: A young goalie in a difficult situation. Felix Potvin, boasting enough honours from Junior hockey to fill any trophy case, was called up by Toronto briefly in 1990-91 before earning a spot the following season, when high-profile Grant Fuhr was injured. Potvin backstopped the Leafs to the final four in the 1992-93 playoffs, losing to Wayne Gretzky's LA Kings is the seventh game of their series.

Mervyn "Red" Dutton and Frank Calder. Born in New York City of Jewish parentage, Bettman was essentially what NHL people would call 'a non-hockey person." During his lengthy NBA stint he was credited with several achievements including the institution of a highly-successful salary cap and the ability to hammer out labor agreements with a minimum of pain. Bettman officially took office on February 1, 1993 and immediately began re-shaping the league high command.

He appointed ABC-TV executive Stephen Solomon — whose grandfather was a shareholder in the New York Americans — his second in command as vice-president and fortified the hitherto neglected public relations bureau with two top-flight executives, Arthur Pincus and Bernadette Mansur. He also made a conscious effort to improve the league's image and rapidly visited every city in the league.

Bettman's appointment coincided with still another landmark decision; to place teams in South Florida and Anaheim, California. To the delight of 24 NHL owners, the Walt Disney Corporation coughed up $50 million and named its club The Mighty Ducks of Anaheim while Wayne Huizenga, father of the Blockbuster Video empire, did likewise for a club that would open the 1993-94 season in Miami but eventually would re-locate at a new arena outside the city.

The idea that the NHL would have two teams in Florida and three in California might have seemed preposterous only a few years ago but the face of big-league hockey was changing faster than anyone could have imagined. The new Lightning club, orchestrated by Phil Esposito and Terry Crisp, became competitive quicker than anyone believed possible and at one point was near the top of the Norris Division. Fans in the Tampa Bay-St.Petersburg communities embraced their new team as did sup-

Above: Adam Oates proved his big point totals in St. Louis were no fluke. After demanding a salary similar to linemate Brett Hull's, Oates was unceremoniously traded to the Bruins. The result: his point totals remained consistently high, his earnings increased, and Hull's numbers dipped dramatically, along with the fortunes of St. Louis.

porters of the equally new Ottawa Senators who, unfortunately, enjoyed little success on the ice.

The same could be said for the San Jose Sharks, in their second NHL season, playing out of San Francisco's Cow Palace. Despite a chronically poor club, the Sharks regularly filled their temporary arena and reaped a fortune marketing team jerseys, hats and other paraphernalia.

Above: Brian Bellows, a speedy forward with a knack for the net, was one of the major ingredients of Montreal's 1993 Stanley Cup victory.

Opposite page: Strong skating Todd Ewen — part of a well-balanced, well coached Canadiens squad.

Apart from the Hartford Whalers, expansion teams and the overwhelmingly powerful Penguins, the NHL featured the kind of parity of which leagues dream. The Patrick Division race remained unsettled until the final nights of the season. There was little to choose between Boston, Montreal, Quebec and Buffalo in the Adams Division and the same held for races in the Smythe and Norris sectors.

While Lindros received most of the early-season publicity, it would be a fleet Finn, Teemu Selanne, who would grab the spotlight as the season reached the homestretch. Selanne would give Winnipeg a superstar of the highest magnitude. He would lead all rookies in scoring (76-56-132) and finish fifth overall in the race for the Art Ross Trophy.

Interestingly, Winnipeg foundered during the early part of the season and it wasn't until a major fight took place that the Jets fortunes changed. The bout, between the Rangers' Tie Domi and Detroit's Bob Probert, had become a cause-celebre after Domi told Toronto Sun sports editor Scott Morrison that he was looking forward to clobbering the Red Wings heavyweight. When the teams finally met on Madison Square Garden ice, the impending collision had become a league-wide story and within a minute Domi and Probert were walloping each other. Probert clearly won the fight while Domi received considerable criticism for his "premeditation" of the bout.

The embarrassed Rangers traded Domi and forward Kris King to the Jets for Ed Olczyk. Instantly, Domi-King brought a toughness to the Winnipeggers that had previously been lacking and almost overnight the Jets became a winning club and Selanne was able to freewheel as never before.

Selanne and Lindros were among many glittering freshmen. Joe Juneau scored 102 points (84-32) for the Bruins while Alexei Zhamnov of Winnipeg and Andrei Kovalenko of Quebec finished fourth and fifth, respectively, in rookie scoring. The Islanders playoff rush was accentuated by stylish Russian defenseman Vladimir Malakhov and his brash Lithuanian sidekick, Darius Kasparaitis. The latter was a throwback to 1940ish hip-checking defensemen such as Bill Barilko and Garth Boesch and became a fan favorite at Nassau Coliseum.

Another headline-grabbing Russian was Alexander Mogilny who scored 76 goals in 77 games for Buffalo and teamed expertly with Pat LaFontaine who finished the regular campaign with 53-95-148, second only to Lemieux's 59-91-160. There was, however, a significant difference; LaFontaine played a full 84-game schedule for Buffalo whereas Lemieux played only 60 games for Pittsburgh.

Just when it appeared that Le Grand Magnifique, Lemieux, would break all of Wayne Gretzky's scoring records, he was diagnosed as having Hodgkin's Disease. It was freely predicted that Mario would never play again; certainly wouldn't return in 1992-93 and, even if he did return, would not be the player he had been pre-Hodgkins. But Lemieux stunned just about everyone. After undergoing extensive treatments, he insisted upon returning to the lineup whereupon he led the Penguins to an unprecedented winning streak that lasted into the final week of the season. By that time Pittsburgh had cemented first place and finished with 119 points, ten more than runner-up Boston.

Lemieux's exit wasn't the only shocker. Brian Leetch, the 1992 Norris Trophy-winner was sidelined early in the season after a crash into the boards at St. Louis Arena. After a long recuperation, Leetch returned to the Rangers' lineup for what the New Yorkers hoped would be a strong run for a playoff berth. But then the most unlikely event thrust Leetch out of the picture. After dining out with some teammates, Brian returned to his Broadway apartment house, stepped out of a cab, slipped on ice and damaged his ankle so badly that he was unable to play another game for the remainder of the season. Not surprisingly, the Rangers finished dead last in the Patrick Division.

The injuries to Lindros pushed the Flyers down near the bottom as well but upon his late season return, Philly turned into one of the league's hottest teams and actually climbed over the Rangers to wind up fifth in the competitive Patrick race. The surge should have been enough to ensure Bill Dineen a return as coach but shortly after the season ended, he was replaced by Terry Simpson. The Flyers had hoped to land Mike Keenan but Iron Mike opted for Broadway and signed a lucrative deal with the Rangers.

Events in the playoffs inspired other changes. The Red Wings, favored by many to win The Stanley Cup, were beaten by the Maple Leafs. Bryan Murray, who held the dual jobs of general manager and coach, resigned the coaching position and was replaced by hockey's winningest coach, Scotty Bowman.

When the playoffs began in April 1993, the Penguins were odds-on favorites to win their third Stanley Cup and their relatively simple five-game series with New Jersey bolstered that thinking. But, already, there were signs that 1993 would be a curious playoff year. Both first-place Boston and first-place Chicago were ousted in four straight by Buffalo and St. Louis, respectively.

What made this even more strange is that

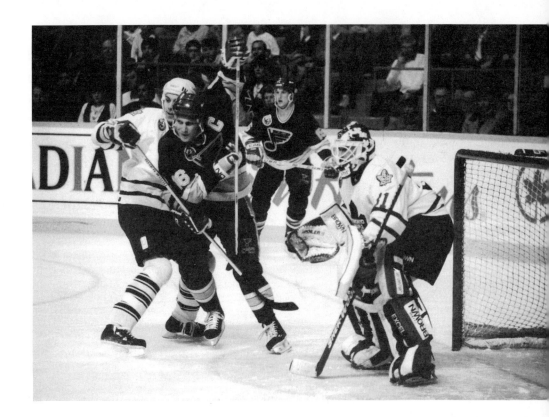

Right: Brett Hull buzzes the Toronto goal. The two teams played one of the longest playoff rounds in NHL history in 1992-93.

the Blues just barely beat out Minnesota for a playoff berth and likely would have missed had the North Stars not been tormented with an impending franchise move from Bloomington to Dallas.

Still another upset was the Islanders six-game triumph over Washington in a series that was marred by Dale Hunter's behind-the-back clobbering of New York superstar Pierre Turgeon in the final minutes of the sixth game at Nassau Coliseum. Commissioner Gary Bettman suspended Hunter an unprecedented 21 games in 1993-94.

Without Turgeon, the Isles were expected to be sitting ducks for the well-rested Penguins. Instead, New York opened with a victory at The Igloo and then extended Pittsburgh to a full seven games. In the finale, the Islanders delivered one of the most unexpected upsets of all time. After falling behind by a goal, the Isles tied the count and then went ahead 3-1. The Penguins made a grand comeback, scoring two

late third period goals to tie the score 3-3. But in overtime, David Volek, who had been an Islander bench-warmer for most of the season, scored the winning goal on a three-man break, taking a pass from Ray Ferraro to one-time a 20-foot shot past Tom Barrasso. Like Humpty-Dumpty, the Penguins had a great fall and the first victim was Bowman who got his release before the playoffs had ended.

The Cinderella Islanders had little time to rejoice. They defeated Pittsburgh late on a Friday night and then were compelled to jet to Montreal to start the Wales Conference championship on Sunday afternoon at The Forum. Although the Isles eventually were defeated in five games they nearly beat the Habs in two overtime games that could have gone either way. Missed chances by Ferraro, Turgeon, and Benoit Hogue proved to be the difference.

To the astonishment of many, the Maple Leafs under coach Pat Burns, continued winning, beating out St.Louis in a seven-game set o reach the Campbell Conference champion-hip round. Toronto's opponents, the Kings, ad knocked off Calgary and then Vancouver s Wayne Gretzky appeared to have regained he form that had been cramped due to back roblems and age.

Many experts regard the Toronto-Los Aneles series as a classic. By this time the league ad set a record for overtime games but they ontinued happening as the series lead moved ack and forth between the clubs.

When the Maple Leafs took a three-gameso-two advantage to The Great Western Foum, Burns' sextet seemed capable of ending he set. But a late third period penalty to Glenn Anderson of Toronto enabled Gretzky to score he overtime winner early in the first sudden-leath frame.

Left: The "Finnish Flash" Temmu Selanne, who shattered all single season scoring records for rookies by potting 76 goals. His scoring pace increased noticably with Winnipeg's acquisition of bodygaurd Tie Domi (above).

Game Seven at Maple Leaf Gardens could have been scripted in Hollywood. The Kings went ahead, 2-0, but Toronto literally roared back to tie the score. Again L.A. took the lead but the Leafs were not quitting and knotted the count once more. With Kelly Hrudey's outstanding puck-stopping, the Kings stayed alive — but just barely — as the game appeared destined for overtime once more. But late in the third period the Kings Mike Donnelly and Gretzky scored a couple of fluke goals. Dave Ellett brought the Leafs to within a goal with a minute remaining in regulation but the Leafs couldn't get the equalizer and Los Angeles advanced to the finals against Montreal.

The Kings advance into the Stanley Cup Finals provided a healthy helping of glitz to the

NHL scene, and not simply because of the Gretzky presence.

Barry Melrose, the long-haired Los Angeles coach, became a sportswriter's dream, and other Kings such as Marty McSorley and Kelly Hrudey achieved near-sainthood in La-La-Land.

Unlike his more traditional colleagues, Melrose had a sermon for virtually any subject and proved to be one of the few people in the universe able to out-talk his voluble adversary, Jacques Demers.

One of Melrose's ploys was to sign on with Anthony "Unleashing the Power Within" Robbins of late-night TV infomercial fame. If a King such as Luc Robitaille suffered a significant slump, Melrose would order a session with Robbins, his personal guru.

Based on the outcome of the final's opening game — 4-1 — for Los Angeles, Melrose appeared to have a Midas if not a psychic's touch. But the Kings' steamroller developed a major glitch late in Game Two. With L.A. leading in the waning moments, Demers fingered McSorley with an illegal stick. Montreal scored on the power play and won the game in overtime.

Pouting over the loss, Melrose snapped. "If I was involved in the seventh game with the series on the line and I suspected Montreal was using an illegal stick, I would not call it. I never did, and I never will."

When the series moved to The Great Western Forum for Game Three, the Habs jumped over Hrudey for a three-goal lead, blew it, and then won in sudden-death on John LeClair's score.

Despite the loss, fan and media frenzy was at an all-time peak in Tinseltown. The L.A. Times put no less than eight staffers on the story, unprecedented for California's leading paper. Former President Ronald Reagan, his

wife, Nancy, and celebrities such as Goldie Hawn and John Candy became front row regulars.

But their support could not get Melrose' men over the hump. Game Four was another overtime affair and, this time, the Kings sent wave after wave against Canadiens goalie Patrick Roy. There were many close calls around the Habs' net but no red light resulted.

In one of their few ripostes, the Canadiens organized a two-on-one break that forced Hrudey far from his net for a save. While the goalie scrambled back to his crease, LeClair retrieved the puck behind the net and caromed a shot off defenseman Darryl Sydor for yet another overtime winner.

The victory was Montreal's third consecutive in overtime in the series and tenth straight sudden-death victory of the 1993 playoffs since the Canadiens lost the opening extra period affair in April.

"It's possibly a record that will never be broken," said Demers. Fortified with a three games-to-one lead, the Canadiens returned to their friendly Forum and disposed of Los Angeles, 4-1, to win their twenty-fourth Stanley Cup, by far the most in the NHL.

Defeat was particularly disheartening to Gretzky who had seen his production plummeted in mid-season only to rise to a playoff leading level during the spring.

"I don't know where I'll be next year," admitted Gretzky, when asked about rumors he was seeking a trade to the Toronto Maple Leafs. "I don't want anybody to read into that statement that I am not happy in Los Angeles or that I want to be traded.

"I'm not sure what I'm going to do but it's time to consider what is best for the Kings and for me. We'll see. It would have been nice to go out on top but who knows?"

Montreal's victory was a triumph for foo

Left: What action! Gritty Canadien' forward Kirk Muller moves into the slot looking for a deflection. Charlie Huddy (22) and Darryl Sydor come to LA goalie Kelly Hrudey's assistance.

oldiers such as Leclair, young defensemen like Mathieu Schneider and Eric Desjardins — he et a record for backliners with a hat trick in Game Two — and of course, goalie Patrick Roy who won the Conn Smythe Trophy as playoff MVP.

It also vindicated Demers, who had coached excellently in St. Louis and Detroit only to be unloaded by the Red Wings in 1990.

If nothing else, the Canadiens' win underlined the NHL's point that a new level of parity had been achieved. Any one of three other virtually equal teams — Toronto, Islanders, Kings — could have won but the champagne went to the Flying Frenchmen.

For the Canadiens, the triumph was deliiously appropriate. It marked the 24th Stanley Cup championship for the Montrealers in the 00th anniversary of Lord Stanley's mug, which had grown to 35 1/4 inches and 31 pounds since its birth a century ago. Demers' outfit, while certainly not the best ever to capture hockey's most coveted prize, did exemplify the best aspect of international teamwork. Their puckstopper (Roy) was a French-Canadian; their overtime hero, LeClair, was an Irishman from Vermont; and one of their best defensemen, Mathieu Schneider, who is Jewish, was born in Manhattan, learned his hockey in New Jersey, and honed it to sharpness in Rhode Island.

At the conclusion of the 1993 playoffs, new commissioner Gary Bettman presented The Cup to Canadiens captain Guy Carbonneau. Bettman's appearance signals a new era in professional hockey, and one which most agree will lift the sport to its highest-ever level of popularity.

Photo Credits

All photos courtesy of Stan Fischler except the following:

Page 17: Photo of the Ottawa Silver Seven, courtesy of Frank McGee Jr.
Page 27: Photo of the Edmonton Eskimos, courtesy of the Edmonton Archives.
Page 56: Photo of Ted Kennedy by Harold Barkley, courtesy of Warwick Publishing Inc.
Page 87: Photo of the Canadiens by Harold Barkley, courtesy of Warwick Publishing Inc.
Page 89: Photo of Johnny Bower by Harold Barkley, courtesy of Warwick Publishing Inc.
Photos on pages 133, 137-155, by Steve Hutcheon.
Photo of Kirk Muller by Dan Hamilton, courtesy of Warwick Publishing.

317410